Praise for *BUILT TO BELONG*

"Natalie challenges us to change our perspectives on business and relationships. If you have a narrative in your head that the other person is your competition and not your friend, that soundtrack is going to encourage you to miss so many new opportunities. Natalie confronts the scarcity and competition mentality head-on in a way that proves there's plenty to go around."

—Jon Acuff, bestselling author of *Soundtracks*

"A call to arms—heart is always more valuable than hustle, and community is always more important than competition. Natalie inspires us to lean into vulnerability and paints a vision for how you can link arms in business and friendship."

—Emily Ley, bestselling author of *Growing Boldly*

"A countercultural must read! Business is all about relationships, and yet we are often in crazy, cutthroat competition with one another. Natalie reminds us that it doesn't have to be that way! We can be successful women with drive and ambition AND still make people our priority."

—Lindsay Teague Moreno, bestselling author of *Boss Up!*

"This message is one the world desperately needs right now. With a heart-on-sleeve style of storytelling, Natalie doesn't hold back—her words are raw, rich, and necessary for anyone who feels like they're wrestling with belonging. Natalie takes you by the hand to guide you with her wisdom and vulnerability. If you're longing for a shift in the way you see and find community, this book is a beautiful first step."

—Hannah Brencher, author of *Fighting Forward*

"Riveting. Relevant. Radical. In a world where people are challenged by the vicissitudes of life and the virus of loneliness, along comes a message in the bottle that simply says we *belong*. Every organization that believes people are more important than profit should consider this book required reading. I am going to recommend it to every leader, individual, organization that I know. A timeless classic that has arrived in the nick of time."

—Dr. Simon T. Bailey, executive coach, author, and thought leader

"Natalie Franke is a champion of people—people over perfection, people over performance, people over competition. *Built to Belong* is both practical and inspirational—an important read for creatives and business leaders about why we should link arms, and the amazing gift of community over competition."

—Jess Ekstrom, author of *Chasing the Bright Side*

"If you want to make a greater impact and find more meaning in life, don't do it alone. Tap into the power of the collective. Natalie's calls to action in *Built to Belong* are the perfect blueprint to widen and deepen your relationships so you can grow your community, business, and heart."

—Antonio Neves, author of *Stop Living on Autopilot*

"An engaging and inspiring read that makes plain the power that genuine human connection can have on our lives and businesses; a fact I've personally witnessed in Natalie's work as head of community at HoneyBook | Rising Tide. The book is an important reminder that we can go further and reach our goals faster when we go together."

—Oz Alon, CEO of HoneyBook

BUILT TO BELONG

*Discovering the Power of Community
over Competition*

NATALIE FRANKE

New York • Nashville

Worthy
Hachette Book Group
1290 Avenue of the Americas, New York, NY 10104
worthypublishing.com
twitter.com/worthypub

First edition: August 2021

Worthy is a division of Hachette Book Group, Inc. The Worthy name and logo are trademarks of Hachette Book Group, Inc.

The publisher is not responsible for websites (or their content) that are not owned by the publisher.

The Hachette Speakers Bureau provides a wide range of authors for speaking events. To find out more, go to www.hachettespeakersbureau.com or call (866) 376-6591.

Library of Congress Cataloging-in-Publication Data

Names: Franke, Natalie, author.
Title: Built to belong : discovering the power of community over competition / Natalie Franke.
Description: Nashville : Worthy, 2021. | Includes bibliographical references.
Identifiers: LCCN 2021010564 | ISBN 9781546017684 (hardcover) | ISBN 9781546017691 (ebook)
Subjects: LCSH: Loneliness. | Communities. | Social media.
Classification: LCC BF575.L7 F73 2021 | DDC 158.2—dc23
LC record available at https://lccn.loc.gov/2021010564

ISBNs: 978-1-5460-1768-4 (hardcover), 978-1-5460-1769-1 (ebook)

Printed in the United States of America

LSC-C

Printing 1, 2021

To Hugh, for loving me unconditionally
and encouraging me relentlessly.
To Mom, for teaching your daughters
that they can rise by lifting others.
To the leaders of the Rising Tide, past and present,
who are fighting for community in a competitive world.
You are the very best of us.

CONTENTS

INTRODUCTION

I'm tired of feeling alone.

The thought poured out of me before I had time to contemplate why. I desperately wanted to pull back those words like a hand on a hot stovetop, but I couldn't.

It was the truth. I hated the feeling, but it was right there—staring back at me with bleak desolation.

For ten years, I had checked off every box, followed the rules, climbed every rung of the ladder as I worked to build my career. And yet there I sat in a darkened room alone…illuminated only by the screen of my laptop, with tears running down my cheeks.

All those goals I had set for myself, all the striving and achieving, had led me here. I had graduated with honors from an Ivy League school. I had turned my passion into a profession and used a camera to create a six-figure wedding photography business that took me around the world. I loved my work and the freedom and creativity it offered.

I had a broad network of friends and business contacts from around the country. I had married my high school sweetheart, and we were looking forward to starting a family one day. I had even discovered the perfect chocolate chip cookie recipe and could make it without burning the edges. I was adulting on all cylinders—by modern metrics of success, I had made it.

I should be joyfully living in my bliss—or whatever the self-help gurus say these days—but I wasn't. I was sitting in my pitch-black office, literally and figuratively alone.

The only light in that dark, empty space that I could see wasn't a way out....It was my computer screen. Thousands of pixels served as both a gateway to the universe and a physical barrier between me and the outside world.

In that dimly lit office, I was a little girl sitting up against the glass window, watching the world go on outside—just far enough away that she doesn't risk getting hurt by the challenges that come with living in community with others but close enough to realize just how much she was missing.

Living behind the screen made me successful in my career, but it also broke my heart.

The painful truth is that I found modern life to be incredibly isolating and competitive. I was communicating with others every minute of every day, and yet I was never truly connected to them.

All of my striving and hustling had left me longing for depth and belonging in what felt like a very shallow world. I needed help understanding why I felt so alienated, so unworthy of love and community. I wasn't sure how to overcome my persistent feelings of loneliness, but I did know one thing for certain:

If I didn't fix this, it was going to kill me.

CHAPTER ONE

BUILT FOR BELONGING

You don't belong.

You are not enough.

You're broken and alone.

They're not your friend—they are a threat.

They don't care about the struggles you face.

Their lives are perfect and yours is a mess.

You are falling behind and falling short.

You don't have anything to offer.

Truthfully: writing those sentences above feels uncomfortable. Honestly, it hurts to read those words, let alone write them.

Why? Because these aren't hypothetical phrases or a made-up list of potential narratives floating around in some theoretical person's mind—these are actual thoughts that I've painfully navigated in my darkest moments.

We need to belong in the same way that we need oxygen—our physical bodies require it. It's knitted into the very fabric of our being. Humans are wired to live alongside others, and not just in some sort of parallel landscape of coexistence.

We belong to one another before we are even born.

Through the blending of genetic blueprints, through the weaving together of two other human lives, our own being takes shape. We cannot exist without the existence of others. There is no me without you.

From that initial spark of life, that first biological blending of our inherited genealogy, we travel into the space that we call home for our first nine months. Nestled deep within our mother's womb, we are connected to her through a lifeline that nurtures our every need. A cord that connects us in the darkness. A cord that remains with us until we meet the light.

> **We belong to one another before we are even born.**

Babies are a beautiful illustration of our biological interdependence.

However, connection doesn't begin and end in our earliest moments. Belonging remains critical in every season of our lives. It is a part of each stepping-stone along our journey of becoming.

In childhood we create friendships in school, and as adults we search for relationships in the workplace. The groups that we are a part of change as we ourselves evolve and grow. People walk in and out of our lives—and some remain for the long haul. Belonging builds us and breaks us. It molds and shapes us. It transforms our understanding of ourselves and others. It is the foundation of the human experience.

Like tiles in a mosaic or musical notes in a symphony—we are separate parts of a collective masterpiece.

We are individual beings existing as a part of a group: a delicate dichotomy between our desire to be autonomous and our inextricable need to be a part of something bigger than ourselves. Within social groups, both humans and other animals battle with the delicate balance between cooperation and competition. The ability to operate as a group is critical to the survival of the species. However, the individual also has a vested interest in being the one to survive and pass on their genetics to the next generation.

Cooperation and competition are a delicate balancing act wired directly into our genetic code. We are built to belong, and yet we are also created to compete. We are constantly at war with ourselves, and it doesn't take much for the balance of power to shift.

When I started my photography business, I dreamed of becoming the best photographer in my city. Years were spent honing my craft, building my brand, and nurturing a client base. I was a solopreneur competing at the top of my game; however, I wasn't doing it alone.

My success was propelled by the success of others. I relied on other photographers to shoot alongside me at weddings. We also shared business opportunities, referring out new clients when one of us was booked. As the photography industry evolved—developing new shooting styles, editing techniques, and marketing strategies—knowledge was also shared, and the collective benefited too.

All photographers compete against one another for business. However, they also deeply rely upon one another. The balancing act between community and competition is a tightrope walk that we must navigate every day.

I have spent years unpacking the significance of this duality—the craving we have to compete and the calling we have for community. This book is my way of sharing what I have learned and elevating the stories of others who demonstrate that we truly can rise together in a competitive world.

For years I struggled to strike the proper balance myself. I wanted to achieve. I wanted my business to flourish. I also wanted to belong to a community whose members truly supported one another.

And I'm not talking about a shallow, superficial type of friendship....I wanted the real thing. I longed for deeply authentic and selfless camaraderie. I yearned for radical kindness—people caring for other people without expecting anything in return. No hidden agendas, no tearing others down, no comparison monsters knocking on the door...I desperately wanted something different.

Yet there I was sitting in the darkness of my office alone—competing, comparing, and scrolling deeper into the void.

There was no single moment that brought me to my breaking point in my battle against loneliness. It was the culmination of smaller moments— times when I felt left out, less than, and unworthy that I carried with me on my shoulders until they brought me to my knees.

Can you relate? Have you ever done the midnight scroll and been left feeling depleted?

Have you ever struggled with comparison or felt like someone else's accomplishments were simply evidence that you were falling behind or not measuring up? Has someone else's prosperity ever caused you pain?

We have been told that in order to be successful, in order to live a life that makes an impact, we must prove ourselves and be the best at what we do. In our pursuit of being *the* best, we lose sight of being *our* best. Slowly we trade interdependence for independence, we choose personal successes over the collective good, and we begin to believe the narrative that it is us versus them.

It doesn't have to be like this.

LONELINESS EPIDEMIC

Loneliness is like a virus. Under the right conditions, a single molecule of loneliness can replicate, spread, and quickly threaten to destroy us.

A virus? How is loneliness a virus?

It is contagious—spreading through social groups from person to person. Its negative effects reach as far as three degrees of separation from the source. The topography of loneliness can be traced through communities, spreading in clusters and wreaking havoc.[1]

Greater sociability enhances brain health and the lack thereof threatens it. Increased rates of depression, cognitive decline, and dementia have been found among adults who are isolated.[2] Researchers estimate that lacking human connection carries a risk that is comparable to smoking up to fifteen cigarettes per day.[3] And many of the studies being done on social isolation are explicitly examining disease-related mortality and thus are not taking into account deaths due to suicide…which is also on the rise.[4]

Atul Gawande, a public-health researcher and contributor to the *New Yorker*, reports that long-distance solo sailors, who commit themselves to months at sea, endure an onslaught of terrors, including raging storms, soaring waves, leaks on board, and physical illness. Yet many recount that the single most overwhelming difficulty they experience is the absence of human connection. It is the unrelenting solitude that threatens to swallow them whole…not just the sea that surrounds them.[5]

Likewise, it is also well noted in scientific literature that the absence of human connection will drive a person to the psychological brink of insanity.

Psychologists have studied this at length by examining the effects of incarceration. In June of 2012, Craig Haney, a professor of psychology at the University of California, Santa Cruz, testified before the Senate Judiciary Subcommittee in a hearing on solitary confinement. With more than thirty years of research under his belt, he condemned this form of incarceration, stating that "solitary confinement precipitates a descent into madness."

In his testimony, he noted that prisoners subjected to long-term solitary confinement endure psychological breakdowns from the lack of human contact. For many, this leads to irrevocable damage, including psychosis, mutilations, and—in severe cases—suicide.[6]

The late Senator John McCain shared about his five and a half years as a prisoner of war in Vietnam—with more than two of those years spent in complete isolation in a windowless ten-foot-by-ten-foot cell. McCain endured repeated torture at the hands of his captors, was denied medical treatment, and suffered from physical trauma ranging from broken bones to horrific bouts of dysentery.[7]

In an interview with Richard Kozar, McCain recounted: "It's an awful thing, solitary."

McCain went on: "It crushes your spirit and weakens your resistance more effectively than any other form of mistreatment. Having no one else to rely on, to share confidences with, to seek counsel from, you begin to doubt your judgement and your courage."[8]

Numerous accounts from prisoners like McCain and others illuminate the horrific damage that occurs to the human psyche in extended periods of complete solitude. Void of any social interaction, we destruct from within.

The sustained stress of extreme isolation damages the part of the brain responsible for learning, memory, and spatial awareness called the hippocampus and leads to a decrease in the formation of new neurons. It also leads to increased activity in the amygdala—the area of the brain that mediates fear and anxiety.[9]

The absence of connection condemns the human mind to a fate that is the antithesis of our very existence. A life of solitude is a psychological path of destruction. We cannot thrive without one another.

We must value connection as though our life depends on it…because it does.

When we are emotionally isolated, lonely, and alienated from the world, we are at risk of losing everything. Social disconnection and perceived isolation is a pervasive problem. The battle for belonging is one waged within each of us, and we are in the fight of our lives.

As you already know, I'm not immune to struggling with this myself. If loneliness is an epidemic, then I am certainly one of the infected. I struggled for years with feeling completely alienated, unwanted, and unsure of how to connect.

Feelings of alienation and unworthiness tormented me…so I dedicated myself to solving this problem. I pivoted out of a successful small business and started building communities across the globe.

> **The battle for belonging is one waged within each of us, and we are in the fight of our lives.**

In trying to cure my own loneliness and cultivate community, I discovered why I had struggled with this from such a young age. Because the barrier that kept me from truly connecting, the obstacle that prevented me from engaging in meaningful relationships, the real reason I rarely felt seen in this world, was my own deeply rooted perception that I didn't deserve to belong.

I felt alienated because I didn't believe that I was worthy of connection.

I felt alone because I didn't feel deserving of friendship. So I went out looking for evidence of these painful perceptions, and I didn't quit until I found it.

Solving loneliness in our lives isn't as simple as joining a community. To truly solve it, we need to first change the way that we think about ourselves and our relationships with others, while truly believing that we are capable and worthy of belonging.

Loneliness isn't merely an isolation problem; it is also a worthiness problem. We must truly believe that we are deserving of love and built for belonging before we are able to receive it.

So how do we get there? I told you that it isn't as simple as building community, so what exactly is the solution?

We must challenge our culture of competition, the societal frameworks and narratives that pit us against one another. We need to stop mindlessly scrolling and start intentionally connecting, leveraging our devices to bring us closer together rather than driving us farther apart. We have to rewrite the relationship rule book together—one page at a time.

COMMUNITY > COMPETITION

There is a better way. And you don't have to do it alone. You can kick comparison to the curb, cultivate a deep sense of belonging, and grow a genuine community of dynamic human beings online and in person.

I've done it, and I'm going to show you how you can do it too.

I want you to finish this book feeling vastly different from the person who opened it. I want you to thrive in a community where you are deeply connected to yourself, others, and the opportunities that exist all around you.

You can carve out a path for your life unlike any other—one brimming with joy, connection, and wholeness. You can fight for others to experience that too.

You are welcome here. You are built for belonging. You are created for connection.

You don't need to spend hours and days and months and years skillfully assembling your mask—creating facades to impress, hiding your scars, camouflaging your exceptionality, and blending in. These modern masks look like virtually curated feeds and perfectly crafted captions. They read like meticulously polished résumés that leave no room for uniqueness— only palatable homogeny in the pursuit of blending in. They are our shields against insecurity and our weapons against letting anyone get too close.

You don't have to hustle, struggle, and strive in stifling isolation. You don't have to carry the weight of the entire world on your shoulders without anyone to help you.

> **You are welcome here. You are built for belonging. You are created for connection.**

I am certain that this reality exists because I've lived it and witnessed it countless times. Over and over again, through loss, through illness, through uncertainty, I have been carried by my community. My life is a testament to what happens when we set aside our culture of cutthroat competition to seek a better way.

Now, I'm not going to say that this road is easy. Committing to changing your mindset and the way you operate is going to be hard. Raising your hand to live a life that puts people first and champions camaraderie means rowing against the current.

However, in order to truly change the way things are, we need to make waves. This doesn't mean that we should eradicate our natural desire to strive for success, but rather ensure that we never seek the destruction of others in the process.

When you walk through the valleys of your life, it can be easy to lose sight of the outstretched arms around you. It can be hard to trust, to believe, to see the impact that investing in community can have when you've grown used to the isolation.

Something powerful happens when you open your heart to the pursuit of doing life with others. Suddenly those struggles that you face are a little less daunting. The weight on your shoulders becomes divided across the shoulders of your friends. They carry the burden alongside you, helping you to make it through each day.

For years and years, I couldn't see the beauty of the relationships that awaited me on the other side of isolation and loneliness. I couldn't hear the voices of thousands of others longing for connection in the chaos. I didn't know that I would one day cofound the Rising Tide Society, a community of entrepreneurs who, just like me, were craving a better, more connected way to live. I didn't know that our hashtag #communityovercompetition would turn into an international movement....

This book is the evolution of six years spent cultivating communities around the globe. We've grown from a hashtag on social media to a community that is inspiring people around the world to reject narratives that pull us farther apart in favor of rising together.

All those years ago, I didn't know how to overcome my insecurities and kick comparison to the curb. I felt alone. I felt unworthy...and it was destroying me.

I know that at some point you have felt that way too.

- Tired of competing and comparing yourself to others.
- Exhausted from the constant hustle to measure up.
- Longing for deep relationships in a shallow world.

This book is my entire heart spilled out onto the page. My learnings from friendships and hardships, from beauty and brokenness. It's a quest filled with vulnerability and a long lesson in embracing my imperfections in order to live a more deeply rooted life with others.

As you experience this book, I'm inviting you to change the way things are. I'm asking you to challenge how you feel about yourself and others. I want you to discover that you too were built for belonging. I want you to walk into a room knowing that you are welcome and feeling empowered to create spaces for others to feel welcome too.

Are you with me?

CHAPTER TWO

MODERN TIMES, MODERN PROBLEMS

Our modern world is a deeply isolating place. It is fair to assume that in picking up this book, you can relate to that...and that a part of you intuitively understands that this isn't the way it is supposed to be.

We aren't supposed to struggle in stifling isolation. We aren't meant to carry our burdens in life alone. Human beings are created to live together—connected, interdependent, and as a group.

Our brains are built for belonging. We are wired to experience pleasure when we are socially accepted and to experience pain when we are rejected or are at risk of banishment from the group. That joy you feel when you're invited to the party and that pain you experience when you see others gathering without you is all by design.

Why? Our ancestors lived or died based on whether they belonged. It wasn't about happiness. It was about survival.

Community is our competitive advantage.

Our brain has evolved under social pressure to make us highly self-aware of where we fit and whether we belong. Social cognition and emotional intelligence are a distinct part of what makes us uniquely human—a consequence of our evolutionary past meant to ensure the survival of the species.[1]

This is no longer the world of early humanity. The way we live, gather, and connect has changed in immeasurable ways. Our neural hardware, however, has not.

The uncomfortable reality is that our brains are wired to thrive under a set of conditions that no longer exists. Our neural circuitry, built to keep *Homo sapiens* alive in early human existence, is now navigating unfamiliar territory that is changing at a faster and faster rate. The world our species once knew would be unrecognizable to all of us.

Think about it: We've traded stone tools for cell phones and slow-paced living for the unceasing rush of everyday life. Information was passed down by generations of oral tradition, whereas now a stream of news updates fills our every waking hour. We've shifted away from communal living into one-bedroom apartments in glass boxes towering into the sky.

The hardware hasn't changed, but the software—the information we're processing and the outputs required for our "mind machine" to operate in our modern world—is vastly different than it was from the outset.

It is important to acknowledge that we brought about these sweeping changes ourselves. Human curiosity led to exploration, innovation, and technological advances that shifted the foundations of society and ultimately changed the way we live and work today.

Community is our competitive advantage.

Technological and economic shifts redefined the household, from generational to nuclear, with more and more people living alone. Human beings went from living in tribal communities where everyone knew everyone to apartment buildings with twice as many people but where we don't even know the person next door.

We used to know the farmer that picked our produce and the family that raised our meat. We would meander through aisles, holding eye contact and occasional conversations, on weekly trips to the market. Now we sit in darkened corners of our homes late at night, illuminated only by the glow of our screens. We choose groceries from an app and peek out of the window as it is delivered to our front porch. No contact needed. The only "connection" required is a strong Wi-Fi signal.

The structural points of interaction that humans relied upon for thousands of years, gone in a matter of decades.

Simultaneously, we've mastered the ability to out-innovate generations before us. Desiring a better life, we have created digital devices that cater to our every need. With proprietary algorithms designed to keep us scrolling and content catered to our individual liking, the world has slowly started to revolve around us.

Every piece of content is tailored to our liking based on previous data we've both intentionally and inadvertently provided. Each suggestion is made with our unique brand of interests in mind. Our social platforms know whether we are conservative or liberal or whether we even care about politics at all. Silicon Valley data analysts know what videos will keep us scrolling longer, so they shift algorithms to increase user retention, thereby driving ad revenues higher and making investors richer. We are too entertained to notice or perhaps too dependent to care.

We don't need to go out into the world searching for happiness when it is hand-delivered to us on a digital platter, right?

This isn't how it has to be. Scrolling in isolation isn't what our brains were built for.

When we look to regions of the world where human beings live longer than anywhere else, we see a uniting set of factors that contributes to their longevity. Eating well and physical activity alone are not enough to sustain us far beyond the median age of survival. It is a sense of belonging and connection to a community that, in combination with a healthy lifestyle, fuels the world's longest-lived people.

In Japan, Okinawans cultivate "moais"—devoted groups of five friends who commit to one another for life. In Italy, Sardinians center their lives around meals shared, often with wine and always with an emphasis on gathering as a family. The world's longest-lived people prioritize connection and have cultivated healthy lifestyles built upon a foundation of belonging.[2]

Additionally, across 148 studies performed on more than 300,000 participants, researchers further revealed that greater social connection is associated with a 50 percent reduced risk of dying prematurely.[3] Building relationships and being a part of a community plays a significant role in our physical health as well.

We understand the benefits of cultivating community and belonging— we know, without needing to see facts and figures, that these tenets are important for our well-being. So, understanding their importance, we try to instill these values from a young age, and yet our competitive culture finds a way to push us in a different direction.

Modernization led us away from the collectivistic ethos that we were created for. We moved away from pursuing communal societies into valuing radically self-centered ones. As a result, the undercurrent of the culture we consume promotes ideologies of scarcity, exclusion, comparison, tearing others down, and winning at all costs.

If we read between the lines in the guidebook to chasing after success, we can almost make out the mantra "every person for themselves."

Just think back to your childhood. When we are young, we learn about taking turns, sharing, getting along, encouraging others, and being kind; however, as we grow older, a slight shift occurs and "winning" becomes more of a priority. We are no longer measured based on our merit as human beings but against metrics that serve to quantify our contributions and abilities.

Grades are given, and academic achievement becomes a gateway to a better future. The harder you study, the better you rank, the more of a chance you have at landing a spot in the next stage of schooling.

Sports teams go from giving everyone a chance to play to requiring players to try out just to make the team. Those who make the cut must still strive practice after practice to stay off the bench.

Cliques form. Classrooms where everyone once felt welcome transform to the mean girls table in the lunchroom. Lines are drawn, and groups are recategorized accordingly.

These early measurements of success, highly based on intelligence, popularity, and physical strength, are ingrained within us as key tenets to strive for. We are compared against our peers and ranked based on how we measure up. Whether directly or indirectly, we are encouraged from a very young age to see our worth and value not in contributions to the collective, but rather in individual performance.

Be the smartest.

Be the strongest.

Be the most popular.

In a culture that glorifies achievement, children are taught to be *the* best rather than *their* best. Slowly, we are pitted against one another as competitors rather than collaborators, as a threat instead of a friend, and in the long run we all suffer for it.

The values of individual performance and competition become more important than the building up of our colleagues and friends. Instead of sharing and collaborating, supporting and inviting, we learn to be suspicious of others, to distrust, and to guard our ideas and ourselves from the community around us. Envy and jealousy are normalized as #goals as we are reminded, almost daily, of who we are competing against.

Mindsets driven by fear and scarcity leave us feeling more and more isolated. We become disillusioned by the everyday grind that has us working harder than ever before but remain detached from what our hearts crave: true community and connection.

These internal narratives slowly weave their way into our daily interactions from these childhood experiences. As adults we long for belonging and simultaneously believe we are unworthy of it. We live our lives in the shallows just close enough to see the safety of the shore without wading out into the deep end.

When we are happy, we fear letting anyone come too close. When we are hurt, we choose to run rather than reconcile. We dodge eye contact and are more comfortable sending a text than making a phone call.

We sum up a person's entire existence into a profile photograph and one hundred and forty characters. Rather than truly get to know someone, we create mental checklists of requirements and read through résumés. We swipe left and right to categorize our potential partners—a lifetime of connection determined by instantaneous judgment in less time than it takes to have a conversation.

And in our pursuit of success, we've become increasingly self-centered and out for ourselves. We rank individual achievement above collective advancement. Have we forgotten the ancestors whose shoulders we now stand on—the soldiers and suffragists, the civil rights warriors and pioneers of progression, the ones who sacrificed their lives for the betterment of the whole? Have we become so focused on ourselves that we fail to see our responsibility to one another?

In our efforts to make our personal lives as convenient, efficient, and pleasurable as possible, I fear that we have forgotten what it means to truly care for one another. We have stopped listening and started shouting, trying to be the loudest rather than seeking to hear all perspectives. We choose defensiveness over receptiveness. Kindness is perceived as weakness, and compassion becomes a trait only to be manipulated for the benefit of another. We run as hard and as fast as we can into our separate corners—polarized without purpose, fighting over controversial ideologies rather than fighting for human lives.

We have lost sight of the fact that we belong to one another. We built our modern world not on the basis of belonging, but with a focus on individual autonomy, personal power, and guided by worldly measures of success.

The unraveling of human connection threatens the well-being of every single one of us. Somewhere along the way we went too far off course. We unintentionally created vulnerabilities in our cultural infrastructure and personal outlooks that enabled a monster of loneliness to creep in and set up camp even in spaces that objectively were constructed to cultivate social connection.

Even with all our knowledge about how people need other people, our modern world is aching for connection in unprecedented ways.

Societal institutions that once served as the intersections of human connection are rapidly eroding. There is a decline in religious affiliation, even among those who were once raised in religious families. The number of adults attending club meetings has dropped significantly. Fewer families are eating dinners together. More and more people are living alone.[4]

Human beings, yearning for connection, turn to online platforms to fill the voids traditionally filled by physical interaction. Modern people set out to find community online without understanding that the platforms created to connect them are also required to generate a profit. This creates a unique problem.

Think about it like this:

We hold devices in our hands that cater to our every need—replacing daily interactions with human beings for digital ones that are algorithmically tailored to keep us scrolling. So, we scroll…and scroll…and scroll, unaware that every notification has been tailored to trigger a dopamine release that keeps us coming back for more.

To fill the void that loneliness leaves in our hearts, we confuse consumption with connection. We observe, we lurk, we double tap and drop emojis into the comment sections of other human beings who are also yearning for connection. Then once again, we scroll…and scroll…and scroll.

With time, comparison becomes an ugly monster that grows bigger with the career accomplishments, alluring beach vacations, perfect family photos, and a thousand other highlight-reel-worthy announcements that we consume on any given day. We see others as having what we want, feeding jealousy and a longing for bigger, better, and different.

What is even worse is that we often begin to see others as a threat. We're excluded or left out, or we're not as smart, as capable, as successful, as the person next door. And so, we claw our way to the top, believing we are on our own to get there and that there isn't enough room for all of us.

Slowly, we become addicted to the very thing that is killing us, our mental well-being suffers, and the battle for connection is lost. The loneliness that follows can be deadly. Unlike the loss of oxygen, which would overtake us rapidly, isolation, and its damaging effects on our well-being, takes its toll slowly.

Our intention, of course, is to expand our friendships rather than lose them. But we are breathing superficial air.

When we use online platforms to consume rather than communicate, we lose our ability to connect with others and our insecurities push us further and further apart. Then we end up curating our realities to impress our friends and hiding the pain that lies behind the screen. Even our vulnerability is filtered just enough so that it generates applause and empathy without revealing too much of the truth.

With each scroll, each passing day, the narrative we are being told about one another drives us farther into our separate corners.

We know that we are built for something better—a life alongside others, working together in the pursuit of a brighter future. Modern life brings unprecedented challenges to our fundamental need to belong. However, we shouldn't give up in the battle against loneliness just yet. There is a way to harness our competitive spirit and still thrive in community with others.

There is a road that leads us back to belonging.

There is a future where we once again rise together.

CHAPTER THREE

THE RISING TIDE

I was raised in a family full of science nerds. Not in the trendy sense, but rather in the data-driven, eats-metrics-for-dinner kind of way.

Mom: nurse practitioner

Dad: nuclear engineer

Grandfather: rocket scientist (yes, literally!)

From the time I was little, I embraced my science nerd identity like a badge of honor. I loved learning about dinosaurs and space. I memorized facts using flash cards and could navigate a calculator with my eyes closed.

I wanted to grow up to be a doctor and follow in the footsteps of my family. That was the predetermined path, and I had all intentions of following it.

However, in my junior year of high school, everything changed. I hit a brick wall in the form of paralyzing depression, and after I struggled for months to claw my way out of the depths of despair, my mom gave me a camera for Christmas.

My fierce, resilient single mother was determined to help me find a way back to loving my life again. Her hope was that a little art therapy might help me to find my way…and in her effort to help me cope, she changed the trajectory of my entire life.

I remember the first time that I held that DSLR in my hands.

It felt so new and unfamiliar. Just a black plastic box with a cheap kit lens, it was covered in abbreviations that I didn't understand. Rotating through the dials, I tried to uncover what each of the buttons signified. I spent hours and hours in my backyard learning to master exposure and figure out the difference between aperture and shutter speed.

Becoming a photographer happened slowly and then all at once. As the days passed, my depression gradually subsided and I reemerged from the fog. That little black box taught me how to create again. It gave me a reason to connect with others.

In a matter of months, I went from photographing flowers around my neighborhood to taking portraits of people at the hair salon where I worked after school as a shampoo girl. After every shoot, I gained a little more confidence.

Within a year, I was photographing portraits for friends and second shooting weddings with other local photographers. I created a website and printed my first set of business cards. My hobby had become a side hustle, and in the pursuit of learning photography, I had discovered a part of myself that I never knew existed.

When I held that camera in my hands, I felt complete. Looking at the world through a lens gave me a new way of communicating. Using pixels rather than words and emotion rather than data, I became a storyteller of a different sort.

In college, my business continued to grow. On Friday afternoons, I would take the train home to photograph weddings. Lugging my backpack and camera gear into 30th Street Station in Philadelphia, I would hop on board a southbound Amtrak train and watch the sunset from the window as the world flew by. Then, on Monday morning before the sun had even risen, I would begin my trek back up to school.

Week after week, month after month, I stuck with it. I spent the weekdays studying art, psychology, and neuroscience at Penn and my weekends wiping away tears during father-daughter dances and trying not to get burned during sparkler send-offs.

I put in the work, both in the classroom and as a budding business owner, until the day came for me to graduate. By the time I held that diploma in my hands, I knew that I didn't want to work for anyone else. Entrepreneurship was calling my name and *Natalie-freaking-Franke* was running toward it, full steam ahead.

I was a left-brained girl in a right-brained world—a science nerd who had fallen in love with the art of photography who wanted to prove that she could build a thriving empire of her own. So, I put my head down and I hustled. When I was done hustling, I hustled some more.

Within a few years, I reached every goal I had set for myself.

From the outside looking in, my life seemed perfect. I was happily married, on track to do a quarter of a million in revenue, speaking at photography conferences, traveling to shoot weddings around the world, and living the life that I had always wanted.

However, on the inside I was falling apart. That deep-seated darkness that introduced me to photography came roaring back. My depression was only painfully exacerbated by my feelings of alienation and loneliness.

I spent most of my day alone in my home office, hidden behind a screen. I would wake up, pour a cup of coffee, edit in front of my laptop until it was time to pour a glass of wine. I would fall asleep to an almost empty in-box before repeating the cycle the following day.

From the outside it certainly looked like I was connected—social media friends and followers cheered my business on from the sidelines. But entrepreneurship is lonely, highly competitive, and cutthroat. There was no escape from the waves of comparison that came washing over me.

There was no running away from the way that business was done.

Don't trust your competitors. They will tear you down to pull themselves higher. Kindness is weakness. As an entrepreneur, you must be out for yourself.

However, I knew that the only other people who could possibly understand how I was feeling, the only ones who had walked a mile in my shoes and could empathize with my experiences, were my competitors. In fact, it was other photographers, creatives, business owners who struggled with the same struggles and faced the same hardships. But why should they trust me? What reason could I possibly give them to join forces together in the pursuit of community?

> I would fall asleep to an almost empty in-box before repeating the cycle the following day.

That night, sitting at my computer, crying in the darkness of my office, I hit a breaking point. I couldn't continue living like this.

The success I had been pursuing, the accolades I was chasing, meant nothing without being accompanied by a deep sense of purpose and a space to belong. I was tired of competing, comparing, and yearning for connection. I was tired of fighting for a seat at the table. I was tired of searching to find my community. I needed something better. All of us deserved something better.

There had to be a better way.

There had to be a way to build a business alongside others—a community that would rally behind one another and fight to see one another succeed. There had to be a bigger, better table out there. And hell, if it didn't already exist, I was going to need to build it.

So the following morning, that is exactly what I set out to do. I took to Instagram with a hashtag: #communityovercompetition.

I asked other small-business owners to use their platforms to elevate the voices of a competitor, to share about someone else in their field who was doing incredible work. One person shared, then another, and another. Within a matter of hours, hundreds of people were using the hashtag and cheering one another on. It went viral.

That conversation continued several weeks later over dinner with my husband, Hugh, and two of our photographer friends, Davey and Krista. We talked about the struggles of entrepreneurship and our similar lonely nights spent working late, alone, in the darkness of our offices. We knew that a hashtag alone wasn't enough, that in order to turn the tide, we needed to make waves.

"A rising tide lifts all boats."

It was my husband who brought up the famous saying, in his best John F. Kennedy impression no less. (I think it was followed by "We're gonna go to the moon" as he lifted his beer into the air…but you get the point!)

The adage references the idea that an

> I was tired of fighting for a seat at the table. I was tired of searching to find my community. I needed something better. All of us deserved something better.

improved economy will benefit everyone involved. When one of us wins, we all win. When we champion small-business owners, when we fight together, we are all better off. We were independent boats in the same ocean. We were a part of something bigger.

In the spring of 2015, the Rising Tide Society was born. The four of us, Hugh, Davey, Krista, and myself, worked together to build a community of creative entrepreneurs determined to rise together in the spirit of community over competition.

In May, we hosted twelve grassroots gatherings along the East Coast. We called friends, one by one, and asked them if they were interested in leading a group.

By June, we published a blog and began accepting dozens of local chapter applications to spread these meet-ups to other cities as word about Rising Tide spread. Requests for new gatherings were flooding in faster than we could sort through them. By the end of that summer, we had groups meeting monthly in cities all around the world.

We had struck a chord. The pain we had been feeling was also being felt by other small-business owners on a grand scale.

A single spark born from loneliness caught fire in the hearts of thousands.

In a matter of weeks, with the help of hundreds of others across the globe, we built one of the largest volunteer-led, grassroots communities of creative entrepreneurs in the world. Community over competition was no longer a random hashtag being shared by a small-town wedding photographer in Annapolis, Maryland. It was a living, breathing movement changing the way people viewed one another and the opportunities that existed to grow together in community. However, not everyone was on board with the idea.

WE RISE TOGETHER

When I first started sharing about the concept of community over competition, I was met with a large amount of skepticism. The harshest remarks often came from business owners who had been in the game the longest.

You see, they had tight-knit circles where only a select few were invited to the table. Even within these exclusive groups, knowledge wasn't shared. Information was kept close to the chest. No one was open about best practices or business advice.

I once had another photographer tell me that she would only teach new photographers who lived farther than 250 miles from her hometown because she didn't want them to eventually compete with her and take away all her business.

Many apprentices were forced to sign non-compete clauses and swear to never start a business of their own. New entrepreneurs were shunned and made to feel scared to ask the wrong person the wrong question. Networking events were about what you could get out of someone else, rather than what new relationships you could form or how you could support one another.

The idea of collaborating and cheering for one another in the entrepreneurial space was a foreign concept. Many people who saw the hashtag were quick to respond with why it was nothing more than a naive dream or an unrealistic vision. You wouldn't believe the number of people who told me:

"That will never work. Competing business owners will never help each other."

"You're naive to think you can change things. Business is cutthroat, dog-eat-dog."

"I'm never sharing my knowledge. If it was hard for me, it should be hard for them."

However, the business world was rapidly changing. It used to be that you needed a fancy degree or a large sum of money to start a successful business. Now all you need is access to the internet and a willingness to work.

The democratization of education, the breaking down of traditional barriers, the shifts in technology were making it easier for anyone to turn their passion into a profitable business. As a small-business owner myself, I believed that we had an opportunity to leave our corner of the world a bit better than how we found it, and along the way we proved that community over competition isn't just a feel-good phrase—it's also a strategic business decision.

This mindset shift applies to far more than just entrepreneurship. In all aspects of our lives, we have the choice of whether to view one another as competition or embrace one another as community. We can see the accomplishments of a friend as evidence that we are falling behind, or we can cheer for them passionately and accept the fact that there is more than enough happiness in the world for both of us.

Choosing to be for people rather than against them changes everything. It impacts the way we view ourselves and others. It changes our focus and shifts our trajectory. It creates opportunities for all of us to rise together.

Business owners who understand the value of community over competition are at an advantage in the marketplace. Frankly, all human beings who adopt this mindset are better off in their personal and professional lives. Below I share some of the reasons why.

They are focused on the right things.

Where your mindset goes, your actions follow.

Have you ever tried to throw a ball toward a target while looking in the wrong direction? It won't travel straight. Your gaze shifts your focus, and that focus turns your shoulders in just enough of the wrong direction to shift the ball's trajectory. The same is true in our personal and professional lives.

A community-over-competition mindset brings attention back to what matters the most. It enables you to keep your eye on the target.

You can't lead the way when you are constantly chasing after what other people are doing. In business, this means keeping your eyes on your customers and your mind on serving them well. In our personal lives, this means remaining focused on lifting others up rather than tearing them down.

When we become obsessed with competing, we lose the opportunity to create meaningful relationships. When we become obsessed with comparing, we forget all of the incredible things we already have that we should be grateful for. By cheering for others and rooting for everyone to make it, we free ourselves to move forward and reach our full potential.

Likewise, businesses that are constantly in reaction mode, constantly looking to the left and right to see what their rivals and their competitors are creating—fail to look right ahead at what their customers need. When you're focused on chasing after your competitors, you lose sight of serving your customers.

Championing others and focusing on what matters most brings success in the long run. Quit the constant rat race of competing and start putting that energy where it needs to be.

They know that relationships lead to success.

Have you ever heard the saying "It's not what you know, but rather who you know"? In business and in life this is absolutely the truth. However, I like to go even further and say, "It's not just who you know, but more important, how you make them feel."

All relationships—personal or professional—succeed or fail based on that simple principle: *How do you make people feel? Does each interaction feel transactional or relational?*

Networking gets a negative reputation for this reason. Traditional networking is about entering a room, shaking as many hands as you can, and gathering every business card you can find. Participants become more focused on what they can get than what they can give, and in the process, people leave feeling used.

> All relationships—personal or professional—succeed or fail based on that simple principle: *How do you make people feel?*

That's why businesses and individuals who champion community are setting themselves up for success. They don't walk into a room looking to take advantage or leverage relationships before they have even been formed. They show up with a heart of service, ready to offer value, provide support, and cultivate relationships for the long run.

They give and give and give, often without expecting anything in return. People leave feeling truly supported because they genuinely were. That earnest goodwill becomes the backbone of their brand.

We remember the people who have made us feel seen, heard, and valued. Likewise, we all remember interactions with institutions and individuals that took care of us when it would have been easier for them to look out for themselves. A reputation is a powerful thing, and relationships are at the heart of how a reputation is formed.

The golden rule in business is the same as the golden rule of life: treat people as you would want to be treated, and success will follow.

They understand that successes are shared.

When you are working in community with others, their successes can bring about a positive impact on the collective. The wins of others drive us all forward.

When you see someone else succeeding and you choose to view their accomplishments as proof that you are falling behind or falling short, you have already lost. That mindset has the power to derail your forward progression and leave you feeling unfulfilled in seasons when you truly should be proud of all that you have accomplished.

However, when you shift your attitude to see the successes of others as proof that there is an opportunity for you to also achieve greatness, you are fueled to continue forward.

This fundamental mindset shift is the difference between feeling discouraged and feeling encouraged by the same piece of information. Welcoming and championing the successes of others opens our minds to the opportunities that exist all around us.

I've seen this in my business as a photographer as well. There were only so many weekends in a year and therefore only so many weddings I could shoot. During my most successful seasons, I would end up reaching quota and started referring out business to other photographers in the area.

> **A reputation is a powerful thing, and relationships are at the heart of how a reputation is formed.**

When my business was successful, I was able to pass along referrals to others in my community and share opportunities. The better I became, the more inquiries came in through my website, and the more business I ultimately had to share. My success became a vehicle for the success of others.

Additionally, the emergence of competitors can create opportunities for the collective by spurring innovation and increasing adoption in the marketplace. Think about electric cars. An emerging technology that for many years was perceived as a moonshot of the environmental movement rather than a highly desirable automotive technology.

Then Tesla entered the scene.

Determined to create luxury electric cars that everyone wants to drive, they set the entire market ablaze. I'll never forget the first time I sat in the passenger seat of a Model 3. Up until that point, I had never wanted to own an electric car. With one tap of the accelerator, my entire view was changed. I could barely catch my breath, it was so fast. I went around telling everyone how amazing it was for weeks.

Tesla moved the electric car market forward substantially simply by existing. The more electric cars on the road, the more people experience them, and it pushes the entire movement forward. Additionally, Elon Musk has kept his focus on creating and innovating rather than competing, and the entire world has been better off because of it.

In 2014, Musk gave up Tesla's patents in the spirit of the open-source movement and for the advancement of electric vehicle technology. Essentially, he handed over his company's proprietary technology and made the argument that patents serve merely to stifle progress.

In a public blog post announcing the move, Musk shared, "Technology leadership is not defined by patents, which history has repeatedly shown to be small protection indeed against a determined competitor, but rather by the ability of a company to attract and motivate the world's most talented engineers."[1]

If Tesla moves the industry forward and increases electric car adoption across the board, they and the world are better for it.

The same is true for small businesses and for our personal lives. Sharing knowledge and increasing access to education raises the tide for all. Innovations made by one create opportunities for the consumer and the industry. There is so much to be gained when we are open to sharing and see the opportunity that exists in a collaborative environment.

Success builds upon success. Opportunity creates more opportunity. Championing others brings about the best version of ourselves.

They benefit from collaboration.

Collaboration is where the real magic happens. In business and in life, joining forces to work with others to produce or create something of value brings about the best in us.

Collaboration by definition is as simple as working together with others to achieve something. Think of it like a potluck dinner. Everyone brings their own special recipe so that the group can enjoy a meal together. The weight of responsibility is divided across the shoulders of a few so that the collective can benefit as a whole.

In the wedding industry, creatives gather together on styled shoots. These fictional weddings serve as a space to test out new techniques, innovate on emerging trends, and learn from others. My friend Heather Benge created an entire community based on the premise of creative collaboration called Styled Shoots Across America.

Frequently throughout the year, Heather organizes creatives together in different areas of the country to create spectacular styled shoots. Florists work with florists and photographers bounce ideas off other photographers. Hundreds of creatives join forces to contribute their talents to the event. And the results are astounding.

The result? Ideas and trends that influence the entire wedding industry for years to come. Many of the images being pinned to newly engaged couples' Pinterest boards originated from one of these styled shoots.

Mastermind groups, brainstorming hackathons, and collaborative coworking sessions have all contributed to many of my own most successful initiatives. Business owners who adopt a mindset of community over competition are open to sharing their ideas, receiving feedback from collaborators, and growing together.

They are deeply rooted.

Relationships are like roots. They anchor us to what matters most and connect us to the sustenance we need to thrive. When storms arise, as they always do, and that wind starts howling, it is our roots that keep us firmly planted.

> Relationships are like roots. They anchor us to what matters most and connect us to the sustenance we need to thrive.

Business owners who embrace this mindset are able to better weather the storms that come their way. People who champion this spirit are strengthened by the support of others on their journey. From personal hardships to global pandemics, we need our community most in seasons of struggle. The more we invest in others, the more we cultivate relationships, the stronger we emerge on the other side of hardship.

Later in the book we will talk about my

personal experiences of leaning on community in my seasons of struggle. The biggest takeaway to prepare for: when we are weak, our community is strong.

BUILDING A STAGE

Ain't got a soapbox I can stand upon
But God gave me a stage, a guitar and a song.
—*Ed Sheeran*

Many of you picked up this book because you're tired of the narratives that pit us against one another. You are—as I like to think of it—in the middle of a bad breakup with our culture of competition.

You keep telling this mindset "it's over" only to pick up your phone the next morning and scroll your way into struggling with feelings of unworthiness all over again. I know. I've been there too.

You're ready to find friendships that feel like home. You're ready to discover spaces where you belong and cultivate connection in your everyday life. And in order to do that, you must choose to pursue community over competition.

You see, a competition mindset tells us to hoard our power. To hold on to our secrets with clenched fists and to fight tooth and nail to protect what's ours. Winning and success are its only goal.

Choosing community means choosing to give it all away—to use our power to empower others. To use our voice to give a voice to those

> Choosing community means choosing to give it all away—to use our power to empower others.

around us. To work from a foundation of purpose, not in the pursuit of popularity or profit.

Building Rising Tide Society taught me this above all else:

The world tells us to stand on a soapbox...but most of us are called to build a stage.

A stage allows us to elevate others. A stage is built to last, to teach, to share with people eagerly waiting to learn. A stage is meant to be shared.

A soapbox, in contrast, elevates one voice alone. It serves as a single opinion, a cacophonous megaphone in a sea of conversation, radiating out into space with the goal of drowning out the rest.

Whether you are leading a community, working toward a better world, or simply longing for connection in the chaos, you have a choice in how you want to build. You can elevate brilliant ideas and shine a spotlight on those who have something powerful to share. You can lift others up. You can encourage and affirm their strengths. You can champion camaraderie and connection.

It all starts by looking our culture of competition right in the eye and saying:

"It's not me, it's most definitely you. *It's over.* I'm done letting you control my life. I was built for belonging and created for connection. I was made for so much more."

Then you lift your chin up and walk right out the door...into the next chapter of your life (and this book).

CHAPTER FOUR

PEOPLE FIRST, OPPORTUNITY SECOND

When I was in middle school, my mother thought it would be a great idea to sign me up for competitive swimming. My father swam in college, and she initially told me that it would be a great way for us to connect and a chance to follow in his footsteps.

Up until that point, I had only played team sports, and my experience with swimming was rather limited. I had spent my summers crabbing off the community pier and running through the waves at the beach. The idea of diving into the pool to race against other people was completely foreign to me.

By joining the swim team, I earned some gnarly tan lines and chlorine-bleached hair that rivaled the frosted tips trend of the 90s. I also learned to strike a balance between "staying in my lane" while allowing the rivalry of the race to push me forward. That first summer swimming competitively taught me a lot.

Unlike many other sports, in swimming your success can be quantified entirely in a single metric: your time.

From one side of the pool to the other, the speed at which you move through the water is the ultimate indicator of performance.

> *Improve the efficiency of your stroke to decrease your time.*
> *Train around the clock to decrease your time.*
> *Shave all of the hair off your body and squeeze into one of those wet*
> *suit contraptions to—you guessed it—decrease your time.*

The true goal in swimming is not to focus on beating the other athletes in the pool, but instead to compete against your own personal record. Every swimmer in the pool is racing against the clock, not one another. Your success is propelled forward by competing not against others, but against yourself.

For a highly competitive person, an Enneagram 3 achiever,[1] who spent her life trying to figure out how she "measures up," this was a powerful concept. Channeling my competitive nature away from external gratification and into internal validation enabled me to rise above unhealthy tendencies. By shifting from looking at others as my measurement of success, there was space to build confidence in my own abilities, while also cheering others on in the process.

Under this framework, the sport was no longer a zero-sum game. If someone else won a race in the short term, it didn't mean that I lost in the long term.

Even in my worst races, there was an opportunity to walk away having gained something. *Did I improve my time? Did I learn something new? Did I overcome a fear or strengthen a relationship with a teammate?* Even in losing, I learned that there is much to be gained.

For those who are naturally wired to compete against others, I have found that there is freedom in working to be *your best* rather than *the best*. Freedom in fighting not to do better than someone else, but rather in the pursuit of improving yourself. When you're working to constantly evolve and grow, you remove the finite nature of winning and losing. You eliminate the duality of the game and begin to look at competition as something supportive of your own personal development.

> For those who are naturally wired to compete against others, I have found that there is freedom in working to be *your best* rather than *the best.*

Swimming was one of my first experiences with healthy competition, and the reason it resonated so deeply with me is because it identified my personal triggers (comparison, always striving to measure up, using others as a benchmark for my own success) and provided a cognitive reframing strategy that empowered me to compete in a healthier way.

Each of us has tendencies and motivations that could lead us down a path of unhealthy rivalry. In order to overcome them, we must better understand what those triggers may be, and that starts by defining healthy versus unhealthy competition.

Competition is healthy when it:

- Occurs on a level playing field with clearly defined boundaries
- Honors a shared moral code, set of values, or agreed-upon rules

- Unlocks personal potential and empowers participants to be their best selves
- Creates a collective experience or unifying tradition
- Strengthens resilience and builds confidence

Competition becomes unhealthy when it:

- Has no clear boundaries (pervasive in all aspects of life or transcends beyond the intended scope of the game)
- Operates unfairly or on an uneven playing field
- Is driven by scarcity, fear, insecurity, or a desire to diminish others
- Creates division, polarization, and isolation; ignores the experiences of others
- Leads to the destruction of self-confidence or self-esteem

Healthy competition in athletics is often modeled through fair play and sportsmanship. In the workplace, it may look like celebrating a colleague who gets a promotion that you wanted or asking for critical feedback to help improve your performance when you fall short of hitting goals.

In healthy competitive situations, when the game is over, we move forward in camaraderie—as one community. There is no residual bitterness or resentment. It's okay to be disappointed about the outcome of a single game, but it doesn't lead to anything malicious down the road. We leave our rivalry on the field.

Unhealthy competition means that we will do anything to come out on top. It puts winning on a pedestal, driving participants to bend the rules and even their moral code in order to succeed. When money, power, or influence are on the line, the scales can quickly be tipped in a harmfully competitive direction.

> Sports: athletes ingesting and injecting performance enhancing drugs; manipulating athletic equipment in order to get a leg up (corking bats, deflating footballs)
>
> School: students cheating on exams or buying non-prescribed stimulant drugs to help improve their scores; parents bribing teachers or recruiters to help their children get into a better college
>
> Workplace: employees sabotaging others to win the favor of higher-ups; looking for shortcuts, hacks, and workarounds that go against ethical standards or corporate policies in order to make more money

When winning is all that matters, human beings run the risk of rationalizing even the most egregious of behaviors for selfish gain. The difference between right and wrong becomes clouded in an arena of unhealthy competition. Do the ends really justify the means?

Additionally, the motivators that shift us into ethical dilemmas or unhealthy realms of rivalry are only exacerbated when we become disconnected from the collective. In isolation, we are more vulnerable to act in a way that pushes our competitive nature in an unhealthy direction.

When we spend more time scrolling and consuming the success stories of others than actually living in community with them through the reality of their situations, social media voyeurism leads us into a downward comparison spiral. The amalgamation of accomplishments that snowball one on top of another would threaten to destroy even the bravest person's self-confidence.

Add in the pressure that we feel to showcase our own successes publicly and the simultaneous fear of disappointing others or revealing our flaws and failures to the world and…well, you can start to see why so many people struggle to move past these mindsets that drive us into isolation.

My greatest weapon against my own highly competitive tendencies is a little mental trickery known as cognitive reframing. Essentially, we transform our way of thinking by identifying a certain train of thought and consciously shifting it toward a different perception of the situation.

Cognitive reframing can help us to turn our unhealthy competitive ideologies into healthier ones that enable us to thrive in and beyond the arena.

FROM THIS	TO THAT
Be the best	Be my best
Beat others	Improve myself
External gratification	Internal validation

THE CASE FOR COMPETITION

Are you trying to tell me that competing with others is a bad thing?

I get this question frequently: at conferences, on podcasts, even when talking to the grocery store clerk, when I'm telling her why I'm so passionate about keeping competition in check.

Simply put, the answer is no. Our natural desire to compete is not, in itself, a bad thing. It can actually be a powerful tool when harnessed correctly.

On a physiological level, competition serves as a performance enhancer.

In the case of my short-lived, middle-school competitive-swimming career, I can still feel the cascade of energy racing through my veins every time I hear "swimmers, take your mark." That "feeling" is the body's reaction to consciously becoming aware of the competition—a neurochemical chain reaction that occurs the moment you realize you're not alone in the arena.

The starting signal of the race triggers your acute stress response—more commonly known as fight or flight. As you climb onto the block beside the other swimmers, your sensory cortex identifies the impending competition and the signal is relayed from your brainstem to your adrenal glands, which respond by releasing epinephrine and norepinephrine.

This gives your nervous system a major boost. A rush of what feels like electricity courses through your veins.

A chain reaction is underway. Your heart rate increases and your blood vessels constrict, diverting oxygen to your muscles in preparation for the race. You pull your goggles onto your eyes and take a deep breath. Your airway dilates to allow more oxygen to rush into your lungs, your sweat glands are stimulated, and your body signals to your tissue to begin breaking down fat to be turned into energy.[2] You reach for the top of the block, and before you even dive into the pool, your body is primed to compete. You are ready for the race ahead.

Competition can arise in so many different facets of our lives. From athletics to academics to career performance, when we are engaged in communal behaviors, we are primed for our competitive tendencies to bubble up.

And again, just in case anyone needs a reminder, this is not inherently a bad thing.

What if I told you that by simply being aware you're competing against someone else, it could change the outcome of your performance? What if by simply being in the arena with someone else, you could be better at whatever it is that you do? Psychologists refer to this phenomenon as "social facilitation," and they have been studying it since the close of the nineteenth century.

In 1898, a psychologist by the name of Norman Triplett noticed that cyclists tended to have faster times when they were riding in the presence of another person rather than merely riding alone. Hoping to test this phenomenon in a controlled laboratory format, Triplett designed a competition machine by building an apparatus similar to a fishing reel and monitored children playing the game alone and in the presence of another child.

The goal of the competition was simple: wind up the fishing line as quickly as possible.

In his experiment, Triplett discovered that many children worked faster in the presence of a partner doing the same task than they did alone, thereby proving his hypothesis that performance is impacted by the mere presence of others doing the same task.[3]

Since the discovery of social facilitation, many researchers followed Norman Triplett and built upon his initial experiment, and the findings are fascinating:

- Worker ants will dig more than three times as much sand per ant when working alongside other ants than when working alone.[4]
- Weightlifters were able to bench-press more weight when competing against others than when practicing by themselves.[5]

Healthy rivalry can create the opportunity for innovation, self-improvement, and move the collective forward. It can refine us, challenge us, and reveal our resiliency. It can bring about new inventions and innovations that can change the face of history. From the quest to find a polio vaccine to the race to space, humans accomplish the seemingly impossible when competing in the arena.

Additionally, some of our best leaders are highly competitive people. Having a natural proclivity toward competition doesn't mean you can't also be kind, empathetic, and altruistic. These are not mutually exclusive traits. It's all about keeping those tendencies in check and continuing to put people first.

Competition rightly ordered looks like:

- Never seeking the downfall of others in our own pursuit of success
- Holding steadfast to core values rather than operating from the belief that the ends justify the means
- Doing the right thing, even when it is the hard thing; operating from a place of integrity when competing in the arena

The word "compete" comes from the Latin word *competere*, which means to strive in common.

What's interesting is that in classical Latin the word-forming element *com-* means "with, together" and when followed by the segment *-petere* signifies "to strive, seek, fall upon, rush at, attack."[6]

Even within the structure of the word "compete," the understanding of togetherness precedes the spirit of rivalry that follows. It is common for people to assume that competition is the antithesis of belonging and cooperation. However, when rightly ordered, the act of competing itself *can* bring people together.

For example: you can't have a game without more than one person participating. Whether it is in the economic marketplace or on a sports field, competition requires cooperation and a set of written (or unwritten) rules that all participants are subject to. In team settings, a shared competitive experience can be a catalyst for stronger relationships and a deepening bond.

> **Competition and community are not mutually exclusive ideologies. They coexist and can build upon one another.**

Whenever I meet another small-business owner, there is an immediate sense of kinship and shared experience. We've both taken risks, worked incredibly hard, and fought to turn our passion into a profitable business.

Competition and community are not mutually exclusive ideologies. They coexist and can build upon one another.

THE MATCH

It was the third round of the US Open, and every seat in Arthur Ashe Stadium was ticketed. The lights flickered on as 23,000 tennis fans flooded through the gates of the arena to watch defending champion Naomi Osaka battle fifteen-year-old phenom Coco Gauff.

For many, this match was the highlight of the tournament—a young rising star challenging the reigning champion. It appeared to be an underdog story in the making.

The crowd's energy was unmistakably in Coco's favor, but no amount of cheering could replace the phenomenal execution that Naomi brought to the court that evening.

The sixty-five-minute match concluded in a devastating loss for Coco. Fighting back tears, the teenage athlete slowly retreated from the court to undoubtedly cry in the locker room, away from the lights and cameras.

As tradition would have it, the victor would then be given a final moment to shine, taking courtside interviews with reporters and relishing in her success that evening.

However, that is not how this match concluded.

Witnessing the heartbreak of her young rival and seeing the tears rush down her cheeks, Naomi did something remarkable. Instead of walking over to the reporters, she walked back over to Coco and asked her to join the postgame interview.

At first Coco resisted, but Naomi was genuine in her offer. She didn't want Coco to walk off the court to mourn her loss alone. She instead used her victory to uplift, empower, and celebrate another woman in the arena.

With the world watching, Coco graciously praised Naomi to the applause of the entire stadium. Then Naomi, when it was her time to speak, searched the crowd for Coco's parents. With emotion in her voice and fighting back tears of her own, she spoke directly to the Gauff family:

"I remember I used to see you guys training in the same place as us, and, for me, the fact that both of us made it, and we're both still working as hard as we can, it is incredible. I think you guys are amazing, and, Coco, I think you're amazing."

In their fiercest season of competition, when the stakes were high and the world was watching, Naomi Osaka used her platform to shine a light on the accomplishments of another woman.

She could have criticized her rival, dismissed the fanfare and sensationalized support for the young star, and shined the spotlight back on herself. As the reigning champion, she had every right to assert her accomplishments and remind the crowd who the best player was that evening…but she chose to take a different path.

Naomi Osaka embraced her success with grace, humility, and empathy—affirming that true champions are not afraid to celebrate the accomplishments of others. She showed the world that being a winner is more about how you treat others than it is about who received the highest score at the end of a match.

In that moment, beneath the stadium lights in Queens, New York, the world witnessed what it looks like when competition is rightly ordered.

On the court, they were competitors.

Off the court, they were community.

Two dualities that coexist in the heart of every athlete—and every human being. The understanding that we can be both competitors and community, in both our personal and professional lives.[7]

Even in the heat of competition

True champions cheer for others. They acknowledge the courage, tenacity, and resilience it takes to step foot in the arena, and they applaud their rivals who are brave enough to play to win.

True champions embrace competition as a powerful and positive force, but they do not allow that spirit to overtake them. They understand that rivalry is healthy when it does not exceed the boundaries of the game. They put people first—in winning and in losing.

True champions rise to the occasion and empower others to rise alongside them. They use their light to brighten the path for someone else, seeing their success as an opportunity to help others succeed.

True champions look past the score, the accolades, the cheers from the stands—and profoundly desire a better world for those who are coming up behind them.

True champions love competition, they do...but they love people more.

Rising together in a world that pulls us apart requires that competition be rightly ordered. It means putting people first, before opportunity. Cultivating a deeper sense of belonging does not require us to eradicate our desire to strive for success but rather to ensure that we never seek the destruction of others in the process.

> **True champions love competition, they do...but they love people more.**

We can compete and revel in rivalry, as long as we put our community first. Competition must always remain rightly ordered.

CHAPTER FIVE

MASTERING OUR MINDSETS

Last year, I was doing a podcast interview with a fellow community builder, David Spinks, the founder of CMX, when he asked me a critical question.

How do you navigate building a community for a group that considers each other competitors?

The heart of the work that I do with Rising Tide, after all, is to bring people together who are doing the same jobs in the same local markets and compete for the same pool of resources. In any other context, a group like that would be more likely to fight against one another than fiercely champion each other's success.

How do we build community in competitive or cutthroat spaces? How do we build a bridge between people who perhaps in any other context would be on opposing sides?

The answer to his question is truthfully quite simple: first we have to change the way we think about one another.

If we want to build communities in competitive environments, we have to shift our mindsets. We need members to understand that they are a part of the same group rather than members of opposing groups. We also need the collective to stop operating from a place of fear and scarcity. We need them to trust and to be trusted in return. If we can do that, we have a fighting chance at turning the tide.

The truth is that mindset is where it all begins. Our brains are powerful. When we believe something, our minds search for evidence to prove ourselves right and diminish evidence that might suggest otherwise. As human beings, we favor information that confirms our existing beliefs.

Psychologists refer to this occurrence as confirmation bias.

Confirmation bias is our tendency to search for, interpret, and recall information in a way that strengthens our existing personal beliefs. Essentially, if we believe something to be true, all our experiences in the external world will be interpreted in a manner that reaffirms what we already thought.[1]

What we believe, we see. What we see, we more strongly believe.

For example, when we view others as competitors, we are more likely to see all of the ways that we are literally and figuratively at odds. We look for and therefore discover evidence indicating that our preconceived notions were in fact true.

They are not friends; they are a threat. They cannot be trusted.

Those competitive thought patterns leave us more likely to behave in a way that brings about further discord. We subconsciously shift our tone, our body language, even our behavior to keep others at arm's length. We close off. We hide our feelings. We forgo vulnerability.

We avoid cooperation or collaboration in order to protect ourselves. It becomes about "me" and not about "we."

> What we believe, we see. What we see, we more strongly believe.

The same, however, can be said of taking the opposite approach. When we walk into the world with a deep and unrelenting belief that we are part of the same group or family, the evidence we see will only serve to reaffirm that assumption.

We have the power to transform our lives and the lives of others by fighting for community and embracing that we are inherently worthy of love and a collective space to belong. While we can walk into a crowded room and still feel alone, we can also walk into empty spaces and cultivate thriving communities that never existed before.

Our mindset shapes our perception, and our perception leads us toward our reality.

This is why acknowledging that we are community before we are competition (as we discussed in the previous chapter) is just the first step. Once we understand this, we must then identify and fight against the underlying mindsets that pit us against one another in the first place.

We have to challenge internal and external narratives that keep us fighting for our own seat at the table rather than welcoming others to join us. We have to squash the whispers that keep us worried that someone else is bound to steal our joy. We have to eliminate the dialogues that only further polarize and divide the collective into *us versus them*.

In order to build community where there is currently fierce competition, division, and distrust, we have to reframe the thoughts that we fundamentally believe about one another. We have to shift our perspective.

INNIES AND OUTTIES

At some point in elementary school, I remember being asked a question that completely caught me off guard. I was sitting on the bench beside the blacktop at recess with a friend when out of the blue she asked me, "Are you an innie or an outtie?"

Wait, what? What the heck does she mean? I looked at her and shrugged.

"You know, your belly button. Are you an innie or an outtie?"

Oh! My belly button!

Before that moment I had never categorized anyone based on their belly button. Truthfully, I hadn't given belly buttons a whole lot of thought at all.

However, my friend's question made me realize something...something that to my baby brain was mind-blowing. There are two types of people in the world: those with belly buttons that go in and those with belly buttons that stick out.

It's kind of a bizarre thing if you think about it.

"I'm an innie," I responded.

She smiled. "Me too."

I guess that made us part of the same team.

The act of creating groups and assigning membership based on similarities and differences is something that we do extremely well as a species.

Why are we this way? One theory is that our early humans lived in small social groups that were frequently in conflict with other groups. It was evolutionarily functional for our ancestors to distinguish members of other groups as different and potentially dangerous.[2] As a result, our brains became efficient at making these distinctions in order to keep us safe from harm.

Psychologists and sociologists understand this behavior through the lens of ingroups and outgroups, a construct most deeply attributed to social identity theory and popularized by the work of Henri Tajfel. Human beings are wired with an ability to quickly identify to which groups we belong and to which we do not.[3]

Where others fall along these boundaries is important to our understanding of whether a person is "one of us" or "one of them."

For example, people who share traits, associations, or belief systems with us are part of our ingroup. People who do not share those traits, associations, or belief systems are part of the outgroup.

In the case of my friend and her peculiar question, we were both part of the same ingroup with our "innie" belly buttons. And anyone with an "outtie" was…well, in the relative outgroup. They were not "one of us."

Where people fall within social group boundaries has an impact on how we think about and treat them. For example, we have a tendency to prefer and respond more favorably to people who are members of our own social group through a practice known as ingroup favoritism. Additionally, we tend to see people who belong to the same social group as more similar than they are in reality, and we tend to judge people from different social groups as more different from us than they are in reality.[4]

These psychological boundaries have a significant impact on how we view ourselves and others, often with negative consequences. Social categorization can establish and exacerbate divisions unnecessarily, fanning the flames of "us" versus "them" and ultimately keeping members of different groups from trusting one another. They can lead to biases, prejudices, and stereotypes. We've all experienced this in some aspect of our lives.

However, this isn't how it has to be.

The thing that is most fascinating about ingroup and outgroup boundaries is that they are completely arbitrary and therefore can be artificially constructed or changed. They are real to us because we believe that they are.

For example, psychologists have determined that ingroup favoritism occurs even on the basis of unimportant or irrational groupings (like whether people "overestimate" or "underestimate" the number of dots shown on a display or even on the basis of a completely random coin toss).[5]

Or in the case of being an "innie" or an "outtie," I had never divided people based on the appearance of their belly button until I became aware of those groupings in the first place.

The most powerful fact in all of this remains that social groups exist simply because we perceive those groups as existing in the first place.[6]

Therefore, redefining our perception of who belongs to our social group and broadening our psychological boundaries has the potential to transform how we view and ultimately treat one another. If ingroups are malleable and expandable, we have the ability to build bridges over the divides that once separated us.

It's like changing my friend's question from "Are you an innie or an outtie?" to "Do you have a belly button or not?" Ingroups are capable of broadening when we change the boundaries.

Let's return to David's original question. How did we do it? How did we build a community for a group that considered one another competitors?

In the case of navigating the division caused by competition, this means shifting our mindset to see all members as a part of the same community rather than individual competitors pitted against one another.

A few ways to achieve this mindset shift include:

- Increasing the perception of similarity among members
- Finding common ground or the space that overlaps between opposing forces
- Working to solve a shared problem (that ideally can only be solved together)

INCREASING THE PERCEPTION OF SIMILARITIES

Increase the perception of similarity among members by defining and consistently communicating what they share. Language is one of the most powerful ways to accomplish this.

For Rising Tide, this meant building our community around the collective identity of small-business ownership and uniting members around our shared core values. We intentionally chose language that acted like an identity umbrella where all members could see themselves reflected underneath.

For example, we use phrases like "creative entrepreneurs" and "small-business owners" when referring to members rather than listing out industry verticals. This creates a collective identity where different individuals (photographers, marketing strategists, graphic designers, and makers) are all united together.

FINDING COMMON GROUND

In the context of cultivating community, finding common ground or the space that overlaps between opposing forces means concentrating on the areas of agreement, interest, and value where we can collectively benefit.

Start by asking these questions:

- What are the areas where all members can agree? (Think about interests, struggles, hopes for the future.)
- How can we concentrate on those areas of common ground and build conversation and value around those topics?

For Rising Tide, this means uniting our members around educational content that is relevant to all small-business owners. We cover topics that are critical to their success and also provide resources that are highly relevant to whatever they are facing in their business during that point in time.

For example, during the Me Too movement, this meant creating a Safe Working Environment clause for community members to add to their contracts to protect them against sexual harassment on the job. During the onset of the pandemic, this meant creating a petition and fiercely lobbying for Congress to forgive the Paycheck Protection Program (PPP) loans and provide financial relief to businesses that were being forced to shut down.

Finding common ground enables the creation of content and valuable programming that gives a unique advantage to members who are a part of your community. It clarifies that they benefit from being a part of the group as opposed to going at it alone.

Solving a shared problem

Nothing brings people together like a common enemy, especially one that they must unite to overcome. This section isn't just the plot of nearly every superhero film ever made; it truly can transform the way competing members unite in community with one another.

When we have alignment around solving a problem that we all agree is important, we are more likely to work together in unison. For Rising Tide, this looks like fighting against the loneliness of entrepreneurship as well as the hardships of running a small business. All members know this pain and all desire to overcome it.

As for defining your common enemy, focus on the following questions:

- What are we fighting against? What is the greatest threat to the collective?
- What are we risking if we fail? How dire are the consequences?

- Why do we need one another to overcome this? Why is together the best way forward?

Answering these questions will provide you with the language you need to communicate in a way that unites members around a shared problem and equips them with the motivation to push past previous psychological boundaries and step into a newly defined community together.

CHOOSING ABUNDANCE

Beyond broadening and shifting our perceived social groups, we had a second challenge to overcome when building a community of competitors. Even when members perceive themselves as a part of the same community, they have a tendency to feel as though they are fighting for the same pool of scarce resources.

It's like when you see someone getting something you wanted and you feel frustrated, jealous, even envious. Those feelings can be exacerbated by a competitive mindset of scarcity.

In 1989, Stephen Covey first coined the term "abundance mindset" in his best-selling book *The 7 Habits of Highly Effective People*. He defined the term as: "a concept in which a person believes there are enough resources and successes to share with others." Conversely, he outlined the antithesis of the abundance mindset—one built upon a mentality of scarcity. In my entrepreneurial journey, I heard countless business owners talk about looking at competitors through this lens.

Mindsets of scarcity run rampant in highly competitive spaces—in business, academics, athletics, and life. Wherever there are limited resources, albeit objectively scarce or perceived to be scarce, humans shift from being open and altruistic to self-preserving and self-serving.

A scarcity mindset says: There is not enough to go around. What is good for her is bad for you. It is a zero-sum game and when you're not winning, you're losing.

An abundance mindset says the opposite: There is more than enough to go around. When someone else finds joy or achieves greatness, it doesn't take away from your ability to do the same. There is success awaiting you, and there is also success awaiting others.

Abundance says that there is room for everyone to pursue their dreams.

A mindset of abundance encourages community and collaboration to rise above competition and creates an environment that invites unity. It stems from self-confidence, is affirmed through core values, and elevates the good in all of us. It means that we can celebrate the accomplishments of others without feeling diminished by their success.

It acknowledges that we are all created with unique gifts and talents that provide value to the collective.

My talents and gifts are different from hers. Her superpowers are different from mine. We can coexist and truly thrive together.

On a practical level, choosing abundance means focusing outward, embracing your unique gifts and talents, choosing the win-win over win, win, win, welcoming change, and championing community over competition. I will explain more about these now.

Focusing outward

Scarcity encourages us to remain inwardly focused—to concentrate on what we're lacking and what we don't have. Abundance shifts our focus outward—to look for ways to serve and to ask how we can help. Businesses that adopt this mindset fixate on serving their customers rather than on chasing down their competition. You cannot lead when you're following in the footsteps of someone else, always fearfully reacting rather than pro-actively creating.

This looks like stepping into a community with a heart for giving, to provide value before asking for anything in return. It means challenging comparison with camaraderie instead. Choosing to cheer for people rather than always trying to get what they have. To center yourself in a spirit of gratitude and appreciation for what you have and what you're able to offer.

Embracing your unique gifts and talents

When I first started in photography, I heard the saying "the riches are in the niches." I assumed this was strictly referencing how a company brands itself to target a super-specific ideal client and quickly learned that this applies to our individual contributions as well.

When we embrace a mindset of abundance, we don't feel the pressure to be everything to everyone. We understand that each person has value to offer the collective, and it is through our uniqueness that the whole is strengthened.

Abundance encourages us to hone our strengths and encourage others to do the same. It creates clarity in competitive fields.

Choosing the win-win over win, win, win

People that operate from a mindset of abundance are all about the win-win. They aren't gunning for the competition, but rather hoping that everyone gets a fair shot at success. They look for moments to come alongside others and enjoy opportunities for mutual benefit.

If scarcity were a kid, he would be the rascal on Halloween who dumps the entire bowl of candy into his own basket. You know the one. Instead of taking a single piece, he sees an unguarded stoop, a giant candy bowl, and takes all the spoils for himself without regard for others.

Abundance is the considerate kid. The one who takes his favorite piece, the one meant only for him, and continues on his way. The kid who has faith that there are countless houses filled with candy ahead of him if he continues putting in the work and pounding the pavement.

Abundance is all about the win-win. Scarcity leaves us chasing win after win after win without clarity or concern for others.

Welcoming change

In an abundance mindset, change is not to be feared. When circumstances shift or problems arise, it brings about new opportunities to discover the good that awaits us. Those with this mindset don't stress over short-term losses because they trust that better is always on the horizon.

It might require a heavy dose of hard work and patience, but nonetheless, there is so much more in store. As a result, they welcome change with open arms and see it as an inevitable part of life. Those with an abundant mindset step into new communities with open hearts. They welcome new relationships without fear of losing old friendships they have built along the way. Love and connection remain bountiful in the present and the future.

Scarcity mindsets are rooted in fear of the unknown. Clinging tight to what feels certain, those with a scarcity mindset hesitate to shift horizons and tackle new problems. Change is often met with complaining, concern, and a reluctance to move forward. New relationships are weighed down by distrust, fear, and uncertainty.

Scarcity asks: What do they want from me? Why should I trust them?

Abundance answers: Connection awaits, and I can't wait to see the friendship that follows.

Championing community over competition

Scarcity wants to push others down. To squash their progress before it takes shape—to prevent the success of other people at all costs. A mindset of abundance is about the art of rising. Improving oneself and therefore gently challenging the rest to rise up too.

Abundance says community. Scarcity says competition. Abundance says there is enough for all. Scarcity says there is still not enough for me.

As we fight for deep relationships in a shallow world, we must also fight for a mindset of abundance and a belief that better awaits us in the future. There will be times when this mindset feels counterintuitive, when it would be easier to keep others at a distance out of fear and when we are encouraged to contend for accolades and beat others in the process.

An abundance mindset doesn't require us to stop being our best or to embrace a sense of false humility in our pursuit of success. Instead, it challenges us to set aside fear and move forward in faith—to believe that we can build a better future, together...and to trust that there truly is more than enough to go around.

Shifting our mindsets has the power to bring us closer together. It gives us a foundation from which we can learn to trust and fight to defend one another. It can take a group of competitors and turn them into a family.

In our homes, our communities, our companies, shifting the culture of belonging will always begin by shifting the mindsets that exist within that space. It means taking a hard look at the way we are wired and evaluating whether we can use those tendencies in the pursuit of building a better future.

Belonging can begin only when we stop viewing one another as members of opposing groups and see the abundance opportunity that exists all around us. Community can thrive only when we broaden the psychological boundaries that pit us against one another and instead fight against common enemies that we have the power to overcome only if we work together.

It isn't easy to do, but it can be done, and it all starts with us.

CHAPTER SIX

DIGITAL TOGETHERNESS

For five years, my husband and I had dreamed of embarking on a cross-country road trip and meeting with our community members face-to-face.

We talked about the idea obsessively every few months, but we never could seem to make it happen. Hugh would research travel trailers, I would get hooked on tiny house living TV shows, we would sketch out our route, but something would always stand in our way.

First I needed brain surgery, followed by a period of recovery. Then we conceived our miracle baby and took maternity leave. The dust finally settled at the end of 2019 (and by that I mean that we finally started sleeping through the night again), and the conversations around this hypothetical road trip resurfaced.

However, something was different this time. We'd survived a hell of a lot in that half a decade, and we weren't willing to let this dream slip away one more time.

So we did the only rational thing that two new parents with an "almost" toddler would do. We sold our house and nearly everything we owned, packed our lives into a rental Suburban, and hit the road as soon as the holidays concluded. And we spent two months driving from Maryland to California—changing diapers in the backseat, testing the limits of dry shampoo, and meeting the most incredible humans along the way.

Small-business owners, creative entrepreneurs, and freelancers packed into coffee shops, parks, and theaters to connect in person. We danced under the stars in Miami, picnicked under the Spanish moss in New Orleans, and hugged more than twelve hundred people from the Atlantic to the Pacific.

Then we arrived in San Francisco—our final stop on our cross-country road trip. That's when it happened. *The pandemic.*

Seemingly overnight the world was brought to its knees, and conversations started bubbling up on the West Coast about stay-at-home orders, travel restrictions, and a widespread public health crisis. We had spent the last seven weeks doing nothing but hosting large groups of people, and suddenly it was no longer safe to gather.

We booked an early flight home as fear was reaching a boiling point on the West Coast. It was only a matter of time before it spread east. We spent our son's first birthday on a plane from Oakland to Baltimore—with a pack of antiseptic wipes and two face masks left over from my company's wildfire preparedness stash.

The world we returned home to was vastly different from the one we had left behind in January. Within a week: businesses closed, schools canceled, and every facet of our daily lives shifted.

Physical distancing became the norm. Masks became required outerwear. Trips outside the house were reserved for essential reasons only.

As the virus sent the world into isolation, it directly challenged everything we knew about community and our sense of belonging. In order to survive, the human race was forced to adapt…and so we did.

ONLINE VS. OFFLINE

What a strange practice it is, when you think of it, that a man should sit down to his breakfast table and, instead of conversing with his wife, and children, hold before his face a sort of screen on which is inscribed a worldwide gossip.
—*Charles Cooley, Social Organization: A Study of the Larger Mind*

You read that quote and thought the author was talking about a smartphone, didn't you? Yep, I did too the first time that I read it.

The truth is that these words were written in 1909 by American sociologist Charles Cooley about the delivery of the daily newspaper.

Yes, the newspaper—let that soak in for a second.

Cooley spent his life examining American society including the rise of competition, individualism, and our fascination with technology. And despite being a sociologist from the late nineteenth and early twentieth century, his words feel oddly modern. Cooley's observations perhaps illuminate our innate human desire to consume information and highlight our natural curiosity to understand as much as we can about the world.

We want to learn whatever we can about other people's lives—to listen with perked-up ears to their tales of triumph and defeat. We need to know what is happening in our community and beyond it. Information is power, and curiosity is a cognitive trigger that keeps us reaching for more.

Our passion for acquiring information reaches as far back as our deeply sacred traditions of oral history. It exploded with the creation of the printing press, and it has continued to evolve with each emerging stage of technological advancement. Today, a single tweet can change history in a matter of seconds, and through the democratization of information, anyone can share whatever they want, whenever they want.

Our desire to consume content is not new. However, the speed at which we are able to receive it, the manner in which we are consuming it, and the quantity of it have changed.

For many of us, the majority of the content that we engage with on a daily basis is consumed through an electronic device, delivered via social media.

It arrives nearly as instantaneously as it is published, and we hold the key to anything we want to know, twenty-four hours a day, in our pockets. As a result, the amount of time we are spending on our devices is rising year after year. According to an online survey conducted by GlobalWeb Index in 2019, adults spend on average two hours and twenty-four minutes per day on social media, which has increased from one hour and thirty minutes in 2012. Currently, the typical social media user is on almost eight different platforms.

Additionally, the rise of esports has transformed the way that people consume content online. When I was growing up, a computer game was something you played—not something you watched others play.

However, due to platforms like Twitch and YouTube, watching video games is now more popular than traditional spectator sporting events in the United States. Young gamers and fans are spending approximately three hours and twenty-five minutes each week just watching esports activity.[1]

That's a lot of time spent on a lot of different forums, which are all vying for our attention.

Our lives now revolve around these little machines, and sometimes we can become seemingly disconnected in the pursuit of discovering information and consuming content.

Think about it.

We open our devices, begin scrolling, and an hour passes in what feels like minutes. Dopamine-driven feedback loops invented by Silicon Valley scientists keep us refreshing for validation—yearning for likes, follows, and fulfillment in the pixels that ignite the pleasure centers of our brain. Over time, we can become reliant on social networks to give us our daily rush of hormones, and we slip into dependency without a second thought.

With each refresh, each new set of notifications, we find ourselves a little more addicted to the virtual world and continue consuming more and more of it.

As a result, our minds are constantly at risk of content fatigue—bombarded constantly from the minute we wake up until the minute we fall asleep.

The struggle of the endless scroll is real.

With technology rapidly changing the way we engage with one another, psychologists and sociologists have raced to better understand the impact of social networks and online relationships. Researchers studying the impact of social media on mental health have concluded repeatedly that increased time on our digital devices can have negative effects on our well-being.

Let's look at a few. Increased time spent on social media is correlated with:

- **Increased depression:** A 2018 study from the University of Pennsylvania found that social media users with high depression scores who were randomly assigned to limit usage to thirty minutes per day significantly reduced their depressive symptoms.[2]

- **Increased feelings of isolation:** A 2017 study in the *American Journal of Preventive Medicine* surveyed 1,787 adults in the United States between the ages of nineteen and thirty-two. Researchers found that people who reported spending the most time on social media had twice the odds of perceived social isolation.[3]

- **Lower self-esteem:** A meta-analysis conducted by Saiphoo, Halevi & Vahedi in 2019 looked at eighty-four studies that examined social media usage and self-esteem measures. They found that, overall, social media use had a significant negative relationship on self-esteem.[4]

And so—just as the science appears to suggest—too much time spent on social networks is always a bad thing. Right?

Not necessarily.

The truth is that not all usage of social media is equal. There is a difference between passive consumption and active communication. There is a difference between enabling social media to be a gateway for comparison and empowering yourself to use it as a vehicle for deep connection. Scrolling endlessly is not the same as engaging in an online community or building virtual relationships.

In 2010, Moira Burke, Cameron Marlow, and Thomas Lento of

Carnegie Mellon University conducted a study to better understand the relationship between social networking and feelings of connectedness. The researchers found that direct communication on social media is associated with greater feelings of bonding, social capital, and lower levels of loneliness.

This was different, however, from users who spend their time on the platforms consuming greater amounts of content. Those participants who consumed rather than connected reported experiencing the opposite effect—decreased social capital and increased feelings of loneliness.

Essentially, if I open Facebook on my phone and scroll, consuming and comparing my way through the day, that behavior will impact my mood differently than if I open Instagram with a conscious intention to communicate with people in my network.

This leads me to a critical question that all of us must ask ourselves.

What if social media isn't the problem?

What if it's the way we're using it?

PHYSICAL DISTANCE

Remain six feet apart.

This single sentence changed everything in the spring of 2020. Physical distancing became one of the most effective ways to flatten the curve of COVID-19 infection, and within a matter of weeks, people around the globe were struggling to cope with their new reality.

However, for thousands of people living with cystic fibrosis, this wasn't anything new. Physical distancing is required as a part of their everyday lives. Pandemic or not, remaining six feet apart is necessary for survival.

If you're unfamiliar with cystic fibrosis, it is an incurable genetic disease that most severely impacts lung function. For people living with CF, impaired lung function caused by a thick layer of mucus enables dangerous bacteria and germs to fester—creating chronic infections and long-term lung deterioration.

In 2013, when significant evidence concluded that people with cystic fibrosis are at increased risk of spreading dangerous bacteria to one another, CF experts published a new set of guidelines.[5]

They may sound a bit familiar:

- Clean and disinfect all surfaces.
- Wear a mask in common areas.
- Maintain a minimum six-foot distance from others with cystic fibrosis.

For a second, I want you to imagine that you've been diagnosed with an incurable disease and the only people who can truly understand what you're going through cannot hug you or gather alongside you in person. Fundraisers are held to support finding a cure for your disease and it's deemed unsafe for you to even attend. When receiving treatment, you must be careful not to get too close to other patients at your clinic to ensure that you don't pass germs to one another.

Everything that the world experienced during the pandemic is a required practice for the entirety of your life. It's a set of circumstances that would leave you feeling isolated and alienated, right?

However, for many living with cystic fibrosis and other chronic conditions, the opposite is often true. Rather than accepting isolation as an accompaniment to their disease, they cultivate thriving digital relationships and grow prospering communities on the internet.

These chronic illness warriors have proven over the last decade that genuine relationships can flourish even without physical contact. In lieu of gathering in person, CF groups developed creative ways of connecting without breaking the six-foot barrier.

Through virtual book clubs, happy hours, and digital girls' nights, friendships formed from a distance. Bonds built that rival even the deepest of in-person relationships, online communities that are thriving. Day or night, through hardship and struggle, there is someone there to support you. It's a powerful thing.

Even in our loneliest hour, someone is always just a keyboard away.

When we first created the Rising Tide Society, our vision was to cultivate in-person relationships, and nearly all of our efforts went into growing local chapters in cities around the world. One by one, we added groups and watched them grow.

I was adamant from day one that the purpose of Rising Tide was to turn online connections into offline relationships. The in-person element of community was where I saw the greatest existing need among entrepreneurs and small-business owners.

> ## Even in our loneliest hour, someone is always just a keyboard away.

In many ways, it was my own struggle with social media and my yearning for face-to-face interactions that drove my decisions to prioritize physical meet-ups over online gatherings. I saw social media platforms as the problem. I was wrong.

Several months after I started Rising Tide, a pair of creatives reached out asking to lead.

The duo, Kait Masters and Kit Gray, met in our Facebook group and connected over a unique shared experience—chronic illness. They recognized that there was a lack of support for small-business owners who were unable to attend in-person meet-ups and networking events due to their health, and they decided to do something about it.

From their leadership, Rising Tide's Creative & Chronically Ill chapter was born. As the months went on, this online group flourished despite not being able to gather physically.

Rising Tide's chronic illness warriors have proven that there is power in digital togetherness. Monthly meet-ups are accessible to all members, and relationships are formed that transcend the Facebook group itself.

These brave leaders directly challenged my previously held notion that in-person interactions are a necessary ingredient in building strong relationships. The depth of their unrelenting vulnerability, the lengths to which they go to support one another, and the unceasing compassion that they give month after month demonstrate the true power of online communities.

The members of Rising Tide's Creative and Chronically Ill chapter live in different states, struggle with different hardships, and own vastly different businesses. Yet their collective experience with chronic illness and their commitment to cultivating an online community creates the environment for deep bonds and a true sense of belonging.

While in the process of writing this book, I scheduled a virtual coffee date with Kait on a Sunday morning. I asked her how it is possible to cultivate such deep and meaningful relationships online. Her answer was simple:

Online community is an innovation,
not an imitation.

—*Kait Masters*

Online community is an innovation, not an imitation.
–Kait Masters

The words struck me. She was right.

Online relationships aren't an imitation of in-person relationships. They can be just as impactful, dynamic, and complex. They can bring an immense amount of joy into our lives. They can help us to navigate painful life circumstances and overcome hardships.

Shared experiences online can even lead to a deeper level of connection than that of relationships offline. When a community narrative is unique to that group of people, they may bond on a level that others in their physical world cannot understand.

For Kait, this meant discovering other people who shared her rare disease: myasthenia gravis. She had plenty of friendships in her local community; however, being able to use the internet to discover and connect with others who understood precisely what she was going through was a vastly different experience.

Leveraging online platforms also gave Kait the ability to become an advocate for change, and through her courage and leadership, she changed thousands of lives.

The innovation of the internet has enabled us to expand our connections beyond geographical boundaries and create a virtual world without physical borders. It has transformed the human experience irrevocably by removing many of the barriers that once held us apart.

No longer are you the only person that you know enduring a particular hardship or who is interested in a super-niche topic.

Twenty years ago, there was a chance that you never would have met another person dealing with your particular circumstances. However, today a support group is only one click away.

Even today, you might be the only person in your town obsessed with balancing trash cans on top of their lids. However, there is a Facebook page with more than 13,000 people on it dedicated completely to the art of the Bin Lid Stand. Yes, this is a real thing.

And it illustrates a very important point. One of the most important sentences in the human experience is: You are not alone.

ONLINE + OFFLINE INTEGRATION

What if social media isn't the problem, but rather, what if the way that we are using it is?

From the time we're young, we're taught information from textbooks and learn from the wisdom of our parents in topics ranging from how to hard-boil an egg to the fundamentals of psychology. However, new technologies are by their very nature…new. Which underscores that our cumulative wisdom about their impact on the individual and the collective is nothing more than an educated guess or a projection of emerging data trends.

The truth is that we were never taught how to leverage the internet properly because when our elders and teachers were growing up, it didn't exist. In this same vein, we don't always have the answers for the next generation because what they are navigating in these earlier seasons of their lives wasn't around when we were growing up.

It is okay to admit that you've never been taught or had the opportunity to truly think about how to have a healthy relationship with the internet. My hope in concluding this chapter is to share a little wisdom that I've gleaned from leveraging these platforms to build businesses, communities, and create deep and meaningful relationships with people all around the world.

Here's the truth: Navigating the online and offline worlds in a healthy way doesn't require separation and balance so much as it requires integration with intention. For many of us, too much time on social media can leave us feeling less than and alone.

I believe that the solution doesn't lie in putting down our devices so much as it requires changing our relationship to them. The internet isn't going away, and we can't expect a digital detox every few months to heal our hearts in the long run.

So how do we do that? How do we fix our relationship with social media and the online world? First, it requires us to stop chasing after a digital and physical separation and start concentrating on the good that comes from the intersection.

Seeking to understand the online and offline integration of our lives requires us to identify the ways in which these worlds are woven together, thereby forcing us to intentionally seek out better ways to leverage technology for the benefit of ourselves and others.

In other words, we need to stop looking at technology as the problem and start seeing it as a part of the solution. We need to pivot our outlook from believing that the internet is an imitation of real life and begin seeing it as a way to live our best life.

This viewpoint makes technology a gateway that can be used to build a better world. We must concentrate on the good that these platforms can bring to our lives and think about how to optimize time spent online to bring about these outcomes.

For example, online platforms and social networks enable:

- Increased efficiency in our everyday activities (work, shopping, heck, even taxes!), giving us more time for activities that we love and for connecting with the people we care about.
- The ability to connect with anyone from anywhere, allowing us

to build lasting relationships that transcend geography as well as societal barriers. We can nurture relationships after someone moves away and make new friendships beyond our existing spheres and communities.

- Opportunities for learning that drive all of us forward. We can learn and teach others what we are learning. Education is out there for anyone who has a desire to access it. We can reap the benefits of that and contribute by sharing our knowledge along our own personal and professional journeys.

Ask yourself this: When I reach for my phone, am I fully aware of the potential good that it can bring into my life, or am I repeating behavioral patterns that left me struggling in the first place?

One of those positive behaviors includes shifting from being passive consumers into active contributors.

This requires us to unlearn our patterns of endless scrolling and to actively engage with our social networks intentionally. Yes, that may mean halting your habit of using your phone as an alarm and making it the first thing you open in the morning. What starts as an innocent attempt to stop the device from ringing turns into forty minutes of watching online videos, bookmarking home renovation inspiration, and browsing motivational quotes. *I'm looking at you, friend!*

How can we be better at using the internet to create a deepened sense of belonging and cultivate true relationships?

1. **Create and connect before we consume.** Try for one day to go on a social network only if you're planning to post or directly connect with another person. Notice how often you

open your apps subconsciously to scroll without any true reason to be there. We must consciously shift our behaviors in order to begin to feel the impact of more positive online interactions. Create and connect first before we allow ourselves to consume.

2. **Set intentional time limits.** Deepening virtual connections isn't about the quantity of time spent online so much as it is about how we use that time. Setting aside intentional portions of our day to connect with others online clarifies the intention of time spent on the platform and prevents scrolling without a purpose. It also makes that time more limited and therefore we are forced to use it wisely. Setting parameters reduces the risk of wasting time and increases the possibility of maximizing every minute.

3. **Create a connection list.** If there are people in your life who you can't connect with in person and you want to build deeper relationships with online, create a simple connection list. Write down a list of five to ten people, and choose one day each week when you intentionally reach out. Many relationships are lost simply because we fail to prioritize them and carve out the time to maintain them. A list and creating habits like weekly check-ins can make a significant impact.

4. **Plan specific online events.** Cultivating a sense of community online requires willful planning and purposeful engagement. Plan virtual events with online friends and get creative with how you make everyone feel welcome and included. Oh, and be personal. Sending a "Join This Event" mass invite is very different from dropping into someone's DMs with a

personal note like: "I have been looking forward to getting some quality time with you. Are you free next week?" The more personal you can be with your outreach, the more the recipient will know that you care about them.

5. **Create online rituals that inspire participation.** Think of cyclical rituals that will keep relationships growing over time and encourage people to engage online consistently. In online community groups, this can look like weekly threads that spark conversation or celebrating certain milestones like holidays, birthdays, or anniversaries. Ask good questions that invite people to engage. Online rituals bond us and create shared experiences within a community.

6. **Ensure accessibility for all.** When choosing how to connect online and when to plan virtual gatherings and interactions, be mindful of the needs of your community and strive to be accessible from the outset. For example: Communication should be improved through translation, transcription, and captioning. Schedules should be aligned to increase the opportunity for live attendance, and when that isn't possible, making a replay available is a good alternative. Being accessible means anticipating the needs of your community to ensure that everyone has the opportunity to engage in meaningful interactions and events.

Engaging with intention has the ability to change our relationship with online communities and can empower us to reclaim our relationship with social media.

As we move forward and the memory of the pandemic fades, I hope we do not forget the powerful lessons that this season has taught us. Online communities are an innovation that is here to stay. My hope is that we continue pushing the bounds of digital togetherness and see it as an opportunity to transform the way that we connect—inviting more voices to the table, creating more opportunity for kinship, and serving needs that have, for too long, gone unmet.

CHAPTER SEVEN

VULNERABILITY IS NOT A BUZZWORD

Wedding planning and inspiration boards—that's how I remember the week leading up to the day my life changed forever.

After seven years of dating, Hugh and I were finally engaged. We met as teenagers in Annapolis, fell in love as high school sweethearts, moved to Philadelphia for college, and had returned to our hometown after graduation.

He was my biggest encourager in those early years of small-business ownership. Hugh put his business degree to good use with frequent strategy sessions around the kitchen table and empowered me as I built my business. We had grown up together. There was nothing that I wanted more than to marry this man.

As a planner at heart, I knew that after our wedding we would start trying for a family. I was excited about the idea—maybe a little too excited, because in my typical overprepared, always looking ten miles down the road mindset, I already had a list of potential baby names stored in a note on my phone.

[*Note: I realize this is cringeworthy and embarrassing; however, a quarter of you reading this have done the same thing. Be honest!]

However, despite looking forward to becoming a mother one day, I had one significant problem....I hadn't gotten my period in more than a year. I was experiencing a few other symptoms, like weight fluctuations, chronic depression, and occasional migraines, so I did the only thing a rational girl would do in a situation like this—I took to Google.

Retrospectively, this was without a doubt the worst possible thing that I could have done. The medical professionals in my family (and most of you reading this) are shaking your heads at me right now, but let's be honest: I was on a quest to prepare myself for the worst-case scenario!

Sure enough, the appointment with my doctor only amplified my fears.

She ordered a blood test that revealed elevated hormone levels and immediately made me schedule a variety of endocrine tests, ultrasounds, and when all failed to find the cause of my hormone imbalance, a brain MRI.

Every day that led up to that MRI, the people in my life did their best to mitigate my anxieties.

As the scan started, the radiologist even joked with me about how they didn't expect to find anything—a "precaution" was what he called it. I remember nodding, convinced that, clearly, he had to know what he was talking about.

Midway through the scan, a voice came over the speakers in the MRI machine informing me that I needed to stay completely still as they rolled me out. The doctor needed a clearer picture, and a nurse gently inserted an IV into my arm with an intravenous concoction that made my stomach turn.

Metal—everything tasted like metal.

That false sense of security in the radiologist's voice faded away. *Something was wrong....I knew something had to be wrong.*

After the procedure, I was escorted to a small room with my mom and that sweet boy who had been by my side for the last seven years. He reached for my hand. I squeezed it tight.

There came a knock at the door—*tap, tap.* The doctor returned, and by his posture, I knew right away that whatever he had to say, it wasn't going to be good.

He sat in an old black office chair and wheeled it in front of an ancient computer monitor. With a few clicks, the doctor pulled up an MRI image of a brain on the computer, looked at me right in the eye, and said, "This is what a normal brain should look like." He pointed to certain structures I remembered studying in college. The doctor took a moment to point out the pituitary gland sitting behind the optic chiasma—the X-shaped intersection of the optic nerves where all visual signals flow toward the back of the brain.

Then the doctor switched to a second image of a brain and pointed, saying, "This is what your brain looks like." On the screen, right in the center, where my tiny little pituitary gland should have been, there was a tumor.

A benign mass nearly pressing against my optic nerves.

It felt like the floor went rushing out from beneath my feet. I stood silently staring at the screen, but on the inside my mind was racing.

That thing is in my head? MY head?

I had studied the brain and knew that any pressure on optic nerves can cause visual changes, even temporary blindness. I also knew that if this tumor was already impacting my fertility, the path to starting our family was going to be harder than I anticipated.

Questions started swirling around in my mind....

What would this mean for my life?
Would I need surgery or radiation?
Would I ever be able to have a family?
Would I have to give up my career?
Why was all of this happening to me?

In a single moment, I went from planning my wedding to wondering what the rest of my life would look like. I swapped storing baby names in my phone to questioning if I would ever be able to get pregnant in the first place. All those inspiration boards, those little worries about flowers and dresses, were gone.

In their place I had a scan of my brain with a diagnosis printed in big bold letters: "Tumor."

What wasn't particularly clear was the course of treatment. Why? you may be wondering. Well...there was nothing immediate that needed to be done.

The mass itself was just teetering on the edge of requiring intervention— nearly pressing on my optic chiasma, a millimeter or two away from disrupting my vision. The hormonal ramifications were also unclear. My hormone levels were off, but we were unsure of whether that was caused by the tumor itself or because of damage already inflicted on my pituitary gland.

My doctor explained that neither the migraines nor the loss of hormonal cycles was enough to constitute needing surgery or radiation. We needed more data points.

He also explained that shrinking or removing the tumor didn't guarantee that my symptoms would fade or that my fertility would return. It wasn't a surefire thing. In the case of removing a tumor from the pituitary gland, surgery could actually make things worse.

As far as he was concerned, the plan was to wait and see.

Yep…just wait and see.

This jarring diagnosis did not come with a clear solution or finish line. That was the first difficult lesson that I learned in this season.

I had to surrender my sense of normalcy and relinquish my perception of control without a clear end in sight. I had to reframe my idea of illness from something a pill or surgery could fix to something chronic, pervasive, and possibly lifelong. I had to settle into the discomfort of this diagnosis becoming a part of my long-term experience, potentially without ever being able to fix the underlying thing that was wrong.

Nothing prepares you for being told you have a brain tumor.

It isn't like the movies. The protagonist doesn't always charge forward with fearless determination and admirable wit.

Sometimes she stumbles, shaken and afraid. Sometimes she tries to hide her diagnosis from the world. Sometimes she believes that if she doesn't admit it to others, she won't have to accept it herself.

For the five years that followed, I kept my diagnosis completely hidden. Only our closest friends and family members who needed to know about my benign brain tumor were told.

As an otherwise fairly public person, I had never consciously hidden anything like this from the people that I loved before. This was uncharted territory. There was so much fear and shame wrapped up in sharing my personally painful and unsettling reality with others. I didn't want my diagnosis to be a burden or to change the way people saw me and the impact I was striving to make.

I longed for a sense of normalcy.

I worried about what others would think.

I feared being perceived as weak or in need of sympathy.

I think, most of all, I feared acknowledging my truth. I was in denial, and keeping this secret meant that I didn't have to face my diagnosis.

So for more than half a decade, my benign brain tumor was something I worked incredibly hard to hide from the world. I covered up my appointments, excused away my migraines, and buried my worries deep.

In order to keep that secret, I created a mask.

Not a literal mask—there were no feathers, glitter, or a masquerade gown to match. I'm talking about a metaphorical mask. One that hides the pain, guilt, and shame that you're feeling on the inside.

Masks are created to not only hide the darkness that lies within—insecurities, pain, and trauma—but also to display a version of ourselves to the world that we want people to perceive. We become better and better at crafting these facades as we learn which parts of our story we want to hide and what will make us more socially accepted. Carefully, we construct a public identity that displays the parts of our lives that we want others to see and hides the truths we wish to keep private.

Think about it. When was the last time you asked a friend "How are you?" and she responded with, "Truthfully, my life feels like it is falling apart. I just started medication for anxiety, but I'm not sure we have the dosage right. The baby hasn't slept through the night in three weeks, so I've been a real jerk to everyone in my life—you know, sleep deprivation and all of that. Oh! And I just found another gray hair this morning, which has me questioning my own mortality. Let's just add on to the list of things I don't love about my postpartum body, shall we! How about you?"

By the time we're adults, we aren't only putting on a mask in our most difficult moments, but we are wearing them to model the expectations, behavior, and "highlight-reel reality" of the world that we live in. We create them for our physical interactions with others as well as in the virtual space.

And because we live a large percentage of our lives online, we have additional opportunities to carefully craft our masks. The internet has created physical distance and therefore the ability for people to pause and reflect before deciding what to share. It also gives us an opportunity to hide behind curated feeds, beautiful photographs, and witty captions. When we no longer have to show up in person, it becomes easier to hide what is truly going on deep within our hearts.

We, as a society, have become cultural chameleons—changing our external appearance for safety, acceptance, and success in a cutthroat world. We develop communicative camouflage to hide what's truly going on in our lives because it is easier to bury the truth than it is to risk ostracism or judgment of any kind.

Even in spaces where we are encouraged to speak authentically, the concept of vulnerability is diluted so that it is still palatable. We are taught to be honest, just not *too honest*.

Vulnerability has been redefined.

Vulnerable *adjective* \\ˈvəl-n(ə-)rə-bəl, ˈvəl-nər-bəl\\

~~capable of or susceptible to being wounded or hurt; open to moral~~
~~attack, criticism, temptation~~
showcase just enough to be perceived as authentic without
truly letting others see the mess, the muck, and the trauma that
you've buried within; a socially acceptable amount of honesty that
won't raise eyebrows

If you could have heard the run-on sentence of fear and shame running through my head during the half a decade that I hid my diagnosis,
you would have been completely confused by what you were seeing on the
outside.

Perception: Married her high school sweetheart. Left a six-figure free-
lance photography career to build a thriving community of more than fifty
thousand people. Moved across the country to pursue her dream job in San
Francisco. Traveled to exotic places, finally discovered dry shampoo, and
was living her best life.

Y'all, my mask looked pretty damn good.

Reality: Worried every single day that she would wake up blind.
Dreaded routine MRIs and doctors' appointments. Struggled with strange
symptoms. Afraid that others would find out about her diagnosis and
simultaneously felt shame for not telling them. Cried every time a friend
announced that she was pregnant. Hated her body for failing her. (Oh, and
then felt guilty for feeling all the above.)

The hardest part to admit is that I became so good at wearing my mask
that sometimes I even forgot what was beneath it. Some days I even forgot
that I had a brain tumor.

My half a decade of hiding my diagnosis ended the day my doctor spoke four life-changing words after seeing my MRI in the fall of 2017:

"I am recommending surgery."

Um, rewind…Surgery? Like, on my brain? You really want to go into my brain?

The walls of the little San Francisco office where I was sitting felt like they were closing in. Halfway across the country from my family, sitting alone in a cold sterile room, the day I truly thought would never actually come arrived like a flash flood.

The doctor's words came barreling into my life, tossing all of my plans aside and leaving a trail of uncertainty in their wake.

We were no longer waiting to see what would happen. We needed to act. Five years of denial, half a decade of trying to push my diagnosis to the farthest depths of my mind, were now over.

"I am recommending surgery. The tumor looks bigger. I truly believe it's our best move."

- Brain surgery
- Six to eight weeks recovery
- Short-term disability
- List of risks and complications

The entire conversation was a blur after those first four words. I walked into what I thought was going to be my routine annual appointment with my neuro team and walked out with instructions for when to schedule surgery to have a benign brain tumor removed.

That mask that I had so carefully constructed to help me cope with the reality of having a brain tumor was no match for this moment—the facade that I had built was crumbling.

I walked to the curb outside the hospital and fumbled through my backpack, trying to find my phone. My hands were shaking as I called an Uber to take me back to the office....No, I couldn't go to the office....I needed to tell Hugh.

Hugh—my stomach dropped.

How could I possibly look my husband in the eye and tell him that our entire world was about to change? He was about to become a caretaker for...a month? Two months? The rest of our lives?

Tears flooded my eyes and flowed unceasingly from the moment I stepped out of the car, walked into our building's elevator, and then through the doors of our tiny city apartment. Hugh was standing in the kitchen preparing lunch.

The minute our eyes locked, he knew.

In an instant, Hugh was across the room and his arms were wrapped around me. Sobbing into his chest, I told him the news. He held me as I cried. I can't remember whether it was a minute or ten minutes....Maybe it was an hour.

There was no more pretending, no more hiding this diagnosis. Surgery meant that our lives were about to change in a big way, and although I didn't know what the future would hold for our family, I did know one thing:

I couldn't do this alone.

I wasn't strong enough to face the future without the support of my friends and family. It was going to get harder before it got easier, and we were going to need a lot of help.

I couldn't bring myself to even write the words down, so I called a very close friend. "Can you help me? Can you get these words onto the page, because I know that if someone doesn't help me, I'll never get the courage to do it."

I read and reread the post a hundred times over. Hours later, I hit publish. Alongside a photo of my husband, I finally opened up about my diagnosis for the first time.

The vulnerability hangover hit me instantly. I set the phone down and walked away. It was done. I was done.

Sharing about my diagnosis was not the brave act of a victorious protagonist pushing past her fears to share her story with the world. It is easy for people to make that assumption in moments like these, but in my case, that's not precisely true.

It took me five years to finally take off my mask, and I didn't do it because I was courageous. I took my mask off because I needed brain surgery.

No…that's not honest enough.

I took off my mask because I was going to need to take a lot of time off from work, and I didn't know how to explain that.

No…still not the entire truth…

I took off my mask because the only thing that terrified me more than telling the world I had a brain tumor was the thought that something might happen to me, and my last words to the people I cared about would have been a lie.

That's not the legacy I wanted to leave behind. I didn't want my fear to have the final say.

So I did it. I hit publish. And in the days, months, and years that have followed, here is what I have discovered:

When you take off your mask and allow your truth to shine through, you give permission for others to do the same. Vulnerability inspires more vulnerability.

People I thought I knew well reached out with their own stories of struggle. Friends who I admired for "having it all together" revealed hardships that I never knew were going on beneath the surface.

> When you take off your mask and allow your truth to shine through, you give permission for others to do the same.

They were human too, just like me.

Message after message came pouring in, and I realized that all along I had known only half the story. There are so many of us struggling in silence because when we look around, the only examples of vulnerability that we see are carefully crafted and curated. We see perfect depictions of everyone else, we feel the pressure to compete and measure up, so we shove our struggles down deep.

But wearing our masks and hiding our hardships only keeps us farther apart. It makes it harder for us to connect, to walk alongside one another, and truly do life together. Barriers not only keep our worries out, but they keep the good from getting in. They keep others from getting close.

By being yourself and telling your story, you will make it easier for others to do the same. Vulnerability doesn't have to remain a buzzword. Vulnerability can become the catalyst that changes everything.

STEPPING INTO YOUR VULNERABILITY

In writing about my experiences with vulnerability, I come to you not as a qualified expert but rather as an imperfect student. I have made more than my fair share of mistakes in struggling to chip away at the temptation to appear to have it all together.

Along the way, I've learned that vulnerability isn't a destination. There is no arriving, only becoming. It's a slow and often uncomfortable journey that we all embark upon in our relationships with others.

Sometimes it can feel overwhelming to see just how forthright and public people are able to be with their trauma and hardship. Sometimes we feel called to share our hearts but are unsure of how to begin. Sometimes we're not ready to open up, and the external pressure we feel to be vulnerable leaves us struggling with anxiety and fear. Sometimes we share what we are walking through and are not met with the kindness or the response we were expecting.

All of these experiences around vulnerability are valid. There is no single path to opening up about what you are walking through—no perfect recipe with precisely measured ingredients and meticulous steps that will get you there.

Three cups of courage

One ounce of emotion

Seven scoops of honesty

A sprinkle of humor

It just doesn't work that way. Vulnerability looks different for each individual person. The depths of our experiences, the spaces we occupy, and the support systems we have in place all play a role in how we engage in vulnerability.

When we choose to be vulnerable, we must do so knowing that we are ready for whatever awaits us on the other side. How other people choose to respond in those moments is beyond our scope of control. This means that we must relinquish expectations and embrace that just as others may not be aware of our hardships and experiences, we may not be aware of theirs. Give grace and be empathetic.

As a student in this process, I have a huge list of notes, messy and muddled after years I've spent opening up and peeling away the masks that for so long I thought would keep me safe. In my experience, I've found success in starting small and flexing my vulnerability muscles slowly over time.

Start with yourself.

Often, in the pursuit of being vulnerable, we struggle with where to begin and who to open up to first. My advice? Start with yourself. Check in with your head, heart, and gut. Ask yourself how you're feeling. Use your preferred method of processing to unpack your thoughts and experiences first before sharing outwardly with others.

When you're ready to take things to the next step, wade slowly into the deep end rather than jumping in headfirst.

When sharing with others:

- Opt for one-on-one, face-to-face conversations when possible.
- Begin with your inner circle and work your way out as you feel more comfortable sharing.
- Do not feel pressured to reveal more than you are ready and willing to; saying no is okay, and moving at your own pace, on your own terms is valid.
- Hold space for others to respond after you've shared your story.

- Respect the vulnerability of others and thank them for having the courage to share their thoughts, feelings, and experiences.

Be comfortable with saying no.

The emotional work that accompanies vulnerability is not something that should be demanded of you. You have the power to choose who is safe and who is not. You have the ability to determine when and where you are ready to step beyond your comfort zone into the unknown.

You are the only one who can determine when it is the right time to open up and when protecting yourself no longer benefits you. Although I will always champion vulnerability, I believe it is up to each individual to determine when, where, and with whom personal information is to be shared.

Honor the vulnerability of others.

Healthy relationships and communities encourage and honor vulnerability. When someone opens up about how they are feeling or what they are experiencing, that is the time to stop speaking and start listening.

Respect the feelings and experiences of others in those moments. Hold space for them. Be attentive. When it is time to respond, meet them with love, empathy, and kindness.

The quickest way to kill vulnerability in a community, company, or friendship is to respond in a manner that makes the contributor feel unsafe, unwelcome, or unheard. Don't leap to judgment or reach for prescriptive advice. Thank them for having the courage to share and encourage others to respond in kind.

Thank you for sharing that with me. I am honored that you trust me enough to be so vulnerable.

The more we welcome vulnerability into the spaces we occupy and the communities we are a part of, the more that people will bring all of themselves to the table, and that is precisely the goal.

Cultivating belonging means seeing others not just for who they are, but also for the person that they are becoming. It is our responsibility to fight for environments where honesty is applauded and everyone feels welcome.

CHAPTER EIGHT

FITTING IN IS OVERRATED

It all started the day my mother marched into the family room where I sat munching on DunkAroos with my chin-length bob and bangs that stretched straight across my forehead.

"You turn that garbage off right now," she hollered as the yellow Power Ranger karate kicked a bad guy. *Pow! Boom! Boo*—and then everything went silent as the screen faded to black.

"That is far too violent. I don't want you wasting your life in front of the television," she said as I pleaded with her to turn the show back on. I dramatically cried out, flailing my tiny arms in the air, but to no avail.

That was the last day I ever watched the Power Rangers.

It was also *one of the most defining moments* of my life.

Look, I know what you might be thinking.

"Defining moment, Natalie? Give me a break!"

There are eyes rolling all over the world reading those words.

Yep, I get it.

Some of you think I'm about to dive into a story about how getting out from behind the screen can change your entire life. Some of you are waiting for a cheesy metaphor to drop, while others are stuck on the fact that I mentioned DunkAroos and now you're cursing me for igniting a nostalgic childhood food craving that will likely last until you finish this book. (I'm sorry about that. Truly, I am.)

However, before you write this off as a story about how a little girl became a more social and connected human being who valued the power of community and learned how to reject worldly values of violence, I want to clarify that this isn't one of those stories.

When my fierce single mother turned off the Power Rangers, she took the remote from my hands and replaced it with the *Encyclopedia of Dog Breeds*, a massive book that she likely bought in the clearance section of the bookstore because no one else wanted to read it.

At that moment, my mother made me a deal. "Once you have memorized every dog breed in this book," she said, "you can watch the Power Rangers again."

That was the day my obsession with dogs began.

I opened the crisp pages of that dog breed encyclopedia and I never looked back. I spent the next few months learning about every different type of dog, its unique characteristics, life span, and personality traits. Something turned on in my nerdy little brain, and I couldn't put the book down.

Even to this day, I can tell the differences between a wolfhound, an otterhound, and an elkhound. I know which dogs thrive while living in apartments and which need space to roam. I can even tell you why your husky keeps trying to run away or why your Australian shepherd won't stop nipping at the ankles of your rambunctious toddler.

As a kid I dragged that darn book everywhere with me. I made lists of my favorite types of dogs and studied their unique personalities. When our family would go into town for Sunday brunch, I played a little game of counting how many different types of dogs I could identify and tried to beat my high score from the week before.

This obsession led to a bit of teasing from my friends at school…you know, the ones who were allowed to watch the Power Rangers.

I quickly learned that it was "uncool" to be the girl obsessed with dog breeds, so I did my best to hide it. It wasn't bullying by any means, just small comments here and there that socially conditioned me to understand that some things were cool to talk about and others—in this case, my obsession with dogs—were not.

So I stopped sharing what I was passionate about. At school, I would nod when friends talked about the Power Rangers….While at home, I would stay up late flipping through the pages of my dog encyclopedia. Day by day, I became a little less myself and a little more how the world wanted me to be.

Can you relate?

From a very young age, our need for acceptance and our fear of rejection dictate how much we are willing to share about ourselves with others. And slowly, interaction by interaction, we begin to craft an external version of ourselves that limits the possibility of being outcast and maximizes the chances of being liked.

We go from running into kindergarten blissfully wearing tutus with mismatched socks and gum in our hair to graduating high school feeling insecure about every single part of ourselves. In the process of growing up, we trade an innocent confidence in who we are for a fear about what makes us inadequate or different in the eyes of others.

We do our best to conform and fit the mold of what others expect to see in us. From the mean girls in the lunchroom to the bosses in the board-room, we learn the art of fitting in.

There is science behind this. In early human history, being outcast from your tribe meant nearly certain death. Humans relied on one another in early societies for access to scarce resources, and being liked and respected meant having more power in the social hierarchy.

In the case of my quirky childhood obsession, the survivalist reference sounds a bit extreme. My life wasn't in jeopardy. No one was going to beat me up for lugging around a big book filled with pictures of dogs, but the sheer thought that they might think less of me because of it…was enough to convince my elementary-school self to leave my passion at home.

Our subconscious mind, correlating inclusion in our social group as necessary for survival, informs our conscious brain to modify our behavior in order to be accepted. If being excluded is unsafe, then therefore it seems plausible that fitting in is our only option to success in adulthood.

A vision is cast of who we should be, and so we fight unceasingly to become that.…We lose ourselves in the pursuit of being liked. Our uniqueness, our bold and defiant qualities peeled away little by little… until there is nothing left but the shell of who we once were. We slowly begin to accept the false premise that we must be like someone else in order to be liked.

Slowly, interaction by interaction, we are molded into a version of ourselves that is more palatable to the masses. In the creative world, we call it selling out. In the human experience, it's often called growing up.

Our world over time tricks us into equating fitting in with belonging—two concepts that couldn't be farther apart. We don't need to conform in order to connect. We don't need to hide our truth in order to be seen, loved, and accepted. We need to find spaces where we are welcome and cultivate those spaces for others.

Ask yourself: Who would you have become if you were never taught to feel ashamed of what makes you different?

Think about it. I want you to sit down and have a heart-to-heart with yourself right now. I want you to uncover the essence of your being that has been buried deep beneath, protected from the piercing judgments of the world.

Who would you be if you hadn't spent years of your life seeking the approval of others?

Who would you be if someone hadn't teased you for the way you look on the outside or for who you are on the inside?

Who would you be if you thought the world would love and accept you for who you truly are?

I want to meet that person—the fierce, bursting-at-the-seams authentic version of you. The quirky, flawed, imperfect human that you keep buried behind the rule book of how you're supposed to act and how others want you to be.

My fear for you is that in the pursuit of fitting in, you will leave the most beautiful parts of yourself behind. That somehow you will mistake the hollow happiness of false friendships for the rich and unrelenting companionship that you truly deserve.

No matter how similar it appears, from the outside looking in, fitting in and belonging are not one and the same. Fitting in means being who others expect you to be. Belonging comes from being who you truly are.

Fitting in means doing whatever it takes to be accepted. Belonging means being genuine even if it means risking rejection.

Belonging cannot be achieved while wearing a mask, hiding your heart, or putting on a show. It is built from self-acceptance and grows when we meet the world as we are—not as it wants us to be.

Chasing the feeling of belonging by mastering the art of fitting in is like baking a cake with salt instead of sugar. It may look the same on the outside, but there is no way that you're going to enjoy it when you go to take a bite.

Fitting in cares about how things look.

Belonging cares about how things are.

In order to find a community where you belong, you must embrace who you truly are, free of shame, guilt, and fear. We have to rediscover ourselves and chip away at who we think we're supposed to be.

This isn't an easy task. We construct our perceptions of self from a young age, and the impact of our external environment is deeply rooted in how we've grown to understand our being. Let's look at it this way:

It's been nearly two decades, and I can still hear the societal mantras of my childhood ringing in my ears. *Be a good girl. Don't rock the boat. Don't make waves. Do what you're told. Color inside the lines. Follow the leader.*

Now that I'm an adult, those mantras consciously sound so different to me.

Be a good girl. *Conform to what a woman should be.*

Don't rock the boat. *Don't assert yourself.*

Don't make waves. *Don't challenge authority.*

Do what you're told. *Be obedient and submit.*

Color inside the lines. *Avoid trying something new; the proven path is the right one.*

Follow the leader. *You, little girl, aren't meant to blaze your own trail. You're a follower.*

These phrases seem so simple when spoken in our early years, and yet it becomes clear that their impact reaches deeper within us than we previously thought. Before we have the ability to determine who we are, many of us are told who we should be. We adopt that narrative as truth without questioning the long-term implications.

I want to be clear about one thing as well. Not all internalized narratives are inherently negative. Amid all of those sayings that are ubiquitous with growing up lies a different one—a phrase that became a hallmark of my own childhood and that I remember framed on the walls of many classrooms in my Catholic elementary school. It is the golden rule.

TREAT OTHERS AS YOU WANT TO BE TREATED

It's a single sentence that isn't so much about our own well-being as ensuring the well-being of others. In the case of discovering a place where we belong, it reminds us that we too have a role to play in cultivating communities where others feel welcome.

We must also fight to create these spaces in our world. We must challenge mindsets that both consciously and subconsciously encourage others to give up their uniqueness in the pursuit of acceptance.

Fitting in means uniformity. Belonging means acceptance and inclusion.

Cultivating spaces where others truly feel welcome means being forced to step beyond what is familiar and comfortable. It requires us to stop talking and start listening. It demands that we default to empathy and kindness rather than defensiveness or resistance.

Fighting for true belonging in our world will require us to dismantle systemic barriers and inequalities. For many, that will mean confronting parts of ourselves that we are afraid to admit are there or acknowledging areas where we have caused harm. For others, that will mean getting the courage to finally speak up without fear of saying the wrong thing or being judged for doing what is right. For some, it will mean leveraging your success to amplify the voices of the unheard—to build a stage that elevates the ideas and contributions of others.

It is the harder journey, but it is the right journey. And I want to be clear, "journey" is an intentionally chosen word.

Belonging isn't a destination. You can't arrive there. It is a long and hard-fought process. It is a daily decision that each of us must make when we open our eyes in the morning, both for how we choose to see ourselves and how we choose to treat others.

Fighting for true belonging means confronting a broken world and building a better tomorrow—together.

SO, WHO ARE YOU, REALLY?

Self-awareness is the gateway to a deep and meaningful sense of belonging and success in life. So, before we can cultivate community or engage in meaningful relationships with others, we must first understand who we are.

There are vast ways of doing this, and each of us has our own favorite tools to dig deep into becoming more familiar with who we are. This might mean taking personality tests like the Myers–Briggs Type Indicator or the Enneagram of Personality. Or perhaps setting aside time to ask yourself a series of questions and consciously reflect on how you feel about yourself in your answers.

Asking critical questions is one of the simplest ways to bring our internal thoughts into the physical world. Up for the task? The steps are simple: guide yourself and, if you are an overachiever, three of the people who know you best through a series of questions.

You can use the ones provided below or develop a set of questions on your own.

Personal reflection questions for self-discovery:

- What is my greatest gift to offer this world? Am I using it to make an impact? How can I amplify that impact and lean into that gifting more fully?
- What has been holding me back? What is keeping me from showing up fully in community with others?
- How do others describe me? What are some of the compliments and words of encouragement that have been shared with me over the last few years?
- What relationships am I most grateful for and why? What is it about those connections that enrich my life?

Questions for those closest to you:

- What is my greatest strength or superpower?
- What are three words that you would use to describe me?
- When I'm having a bad day, what is one thing that you want me to remember?

Sometimes we overlook what we have to offer this world because we fail to see the extraordinary in what we've been conditioned to believe is ordinary. We are so quick to write off our gifts as insignificant or diminish our abilities out of fear that somehow they don't qualify.

It wasn't until I asked my husband a single question that I discovered this for myself.

Me: What is my superpower? You know, my greatest strength?

Hugh: You love people well. You see the best in them. That is
your superpower. It sometimes gets you hurt, you know,
when people take advantage of your kindness, but it's
because you genuinely care about others, because you
genuinely believe the best in them, that you are so good at
what you do.

I need to be honest with you—I wasn't loving his answer. *I see the good in people?* That's what he thought was my greatest strength.

I'll admit, I was hoping he would say something about my insane levels of creativity or my rock-star communications skills. Perhaps he would tell me that I work harder than anyone he knows, that I never quit. I'm not sure what I expected, but it definitely wasn't that.

In his eyes, my superpower was my ability to love others and see the best in them. He knew all my strengths and chose to call out that superpower because it was the quality that he believed enabled me to make the greatest impact on others.

He reminded me that my superpower is not insignificant. I had turned my strength into one of the largest grassroots communities of creative entrepreneurs in the world. By leveraging the gift of loving people well, I was able to empower and unite tens of thousands of people from completely different walks of life.

This simple question unlocked a deeper understanding of who I am and what I have to offer. It also taught me that our superpowers aren't always what we expect.

WHEN 1 + 1 = 3

On a late San Francisco summer night, my best friend Rebecca, my husband, and I were having one of our weekly pizza and wine dinners when she brought up a concept that she had been wrestling with for weeks. As entrepreneurs, we would frequently bounce ideas off each other, but this night she was particularly fired up. About what? I wasn't sure.

With a warm slice of pizza in hand, she leaned in and asked, "What if email marketing was as simple as posting to social media?"

"Go on…" I nodded.

"What if there was a way to democratize the design process so that anyone—and I mean anyone—could create a high-converting and aesthetically pleasing email campaign. What if it could look like you have an entire development and design team crafting your emails, but really…it's just you."

Now, before we go any further, I need you to understand that this is how Rebecca talks all the time. Yes, even over a bottle of wine. My best friend runs on a remarkable level of philosophical thought and creative vision.

Rebecca Shostak was raised in Silicon Valley. A design genius whose weapons of choice are a full suite of Adobe, a glass of red wine, and a yearly pass to the MoMA, she's 100 percent introverted and would be perfectly happy dominating the world from behind her laptop.

She is left-handed, red-haired, and within five minutes of meeting her, I realized that she was one of the most unique and remarkable people I had ever met.

In addition to all of that, Rebecca is a design virtuoso. She went from creating merchandise for bands like Linkin Park and Rihanna to building a successful online design and template business that helped create other multimillion-dollar businesses.

She sees the world differently, and as a result, Rebecca often sees opportunities and patterns of behavior that the rest of us miss. Her superpower is her creativity and imagination—matched only by her esoteric intellectualism, which, as a fellow nerd, I admired from day one.

As we sat side by side in my tiny apartment kitchen that night, Rebecca reached for her notebook. With giddy enthusiasm, she started flipping through the pages filled with scribbles and blotches of black ink. One page after another revealed her vision for creating a brand-new email marketing platform unlike anything that I had ever seen before.

My friend had built an entire piece of software in her mind, and seeing her flex her genius was astounding. There was an incredible amount of untapped potential just sitting there. Her idea was a spark waiting to be ignited into a roaring fire.

Rebecca was an architect in need of a builder.

That's where my other friend, and colleague, Martha came in.

Everyone remembers the first time they meet Martha Bitar. The queen of sales with a magnetic personality, this petite powerhouse can walk into any room and immediately woo all in attendance. Raised in Mexico and educated in Texas, she will drop a y'all and then proceed to switch into fluent Spanish…or any of the other five languages she speaks.

You might think that at four foot eleven, she would be easily overlooked in a crowded room, but you would be sorely mistaken. Martha has cracked the code to creating deep, meaningful connections in a matter of minutes with nearly anyone she meets. She is at home in the world, never staying in one place for long. She's lived in Paris and Dubai; she's traveled across Europe, Asia, and the Middle East.

Oh, and with years of sales training, she has mastered the art of convincing anyone to do just about anything.

To put it in perspective, Martha convinced my husband and me to move across the country and take the greatest career risk of our lives—selling our company to a start-up in California. All it took was a good brunch, a scavenger hunt, and a single conversation about the possibility of what could be. Martha is impressive, inspiring, and a force of nature.

Martha and Rebecca grabbed a few drinks after work, and that notebook full of ideas became the road map to building the emailing marketing company Flodesk.

Rebecca's design genius and product prowess combined with Martha's magnetic people skills and sheer willpower were the perfect mix. They took the concept from ideation to beta launch within a year and then proceeded to bootstrap the business while scaling rapidly.

Through every bump in the road and every start-up challenge, they found a way to lean on each other. Apart, they couldn't be more different. However, together they were able to amplify each other's strengths and turn an idea into a seven-figure business in under a year.

Today that company impacts the way tens of thousands of small businesses market themselves online. Isn't that wild?

Apart these two women were successful in their own right. However, *together, they became unstoppable.*

Earlier in the book, we talked about the scientifically proven possibility of increased performance when two competitors are in the arena together. Well, I believe that in business, the same can be said for partners or collaborators joining forces.

When we don't shy away from our distinct abilities, when we stop being afraid of standing out and sharing our unique gifts, that is when others can see how to come alongside us and amplify our impact.

By holding back, by being afraid to truly be ourselves, we fail to create space for our talents to be multiplied. Martha and Rebecca are proof that there is power in collaboration when we accept one another's distinct gifts and talents.

In the intersection where one person's weakness meets another's strength, there lies the potential to amplify our collective power. That's when one plus one suddenly equals three. That's when a notebook full of ideas turns into something so much greater.

When we embrace who we are and accept one another for our differences, the collective is strengthened. Just as you can't create an exquisite dinner with only one ingredient, you can't build a strong company or cultivate a thriving community when everyone is exactly the same.

Uniqueness is not weakness. When we understand how we are each individually wired, we lay down our weapons of competition and comparison to discover that everyone has a role that *only* they can play.

Our individual differences are a strength to the collective, not a weakness. When we aim to fit in, we fail to honor our uniqueness and how it can complement a community, a company, or our collective world. We find greater satisfaction in our work and in our relationships when we are living as our truest selves, and we fight for others to have that same opportunity.

Belonging isn't built in a day, and it isn't a place where we suddenly arrive. It is a daily decision and a battle worth fighting—for you, for me, and for the collective.

CHAPTER NINE

STRONGEST IN THE STRUGGLE

Beep—Beep—Beeeeeeeep!

The glaring white lights of the recovery room dangled above as my head throbbed. My eyes opened, and immediately I could tell that something was wrong.

I was thirsty. That was the last sensation I'd expected to feel as I regained consciousness after brain surgery—maybe a headache or some dizziness, but instead I was unbearably thirsty. In the span of six hours, I had turned into one of those baby vampires whose entire world revolved around getting another drink.

It was all consuming, unrelenting, and nearly incapacitating.

Oh, and before you think I'm overreacting, I'm not talking about your average experience with thirst. This is not the feeling you get when you're overdue for a glass of water or just finished working out in the summer sun. I'm talking about not being able to swallow because your entire throat feels like it has disintegrated into grains of sand after spending three hundred years baking in the heat on the driest place on earth thirsty. Like Walter White in *Breaking Bad* after traversing the entire New Mexico desert while on the brink of death thirsty.

And in my daze of early consciousness, there was only one thing that I believed would come close to quenching that unbearable sensation…a juicy Popsicle.

I know…I know…It's strange. I fumbled with the bedside remote and awkwardly pushed the call button. *rinnnnnnnng!*

A kind nurse entered the curtained-off room, and I begged her to find me a Popsicle. A strange request, but it was the only thing in the world that I wanted and, well, I had just come out of brain surgery, so she seemed sympathetic to my bizarre craving.

"I'll be right back, dear," she responded.

I reached into my mouth, worried that my tongue had somehow dried up and fallen off. Nope, it was still there. *False alarm.*

I guess this is a normal part of waking up from surgery…probably no big deal…Maybe it has something to do with being intubated, I thought to myself. Before brain surgery, I hadn't so much as had my wisdom teeth out or broken a bone.

This was my first time under anesthesia, so what did I know?

In a few minutes, the nurse returned carrying three bright-red cherry Popsicle sticks. *My savior!* She unwrapped the first Popsicle, and I couldn't eat it quickly enough.…

In my uncoordinated post-surgery state, I inhaled it. Red icy Popsicle went dripping onto my hospital gown, running down my face and hands. Small chunks broke off and fell into my braided hair. It was everywhere.

It felt like the only thing keeping me alive was that darn Popsicle. Finishing the final bite, I set the stick aside. *One Popsicle down…two to go…*

That's when the curtain swung open. Hugh and my mom had finally made it up to the recovery room. I smiled a big goofy grin. It was so good to see them.

The look on my husband's face was one I had never seen before. It wasn't happiness to see me or relief that I was okay....No, it was horror.

My husband looked absolutely horrified. Expecting to see me peacefully resting after surgery, my husband instead walked in on his wife covered in red sticky liquid that appeared to be gushing from her mouth. It was like a scene from a horror movie.

Hugh's face went flush, and his eyes darted around the room for the nurse. I could see the situation unfolding faster than I could respond to stop it.

"Uh, is that blood?" he asked.

The nurse laughed. "That's a Popsicle. She asked for it!"

Color slowly returned to his cheeks as he sat down next to me. When he tried to clean me up with a napkin, I brushed his hand aside and abruptly reached for the next Popsicle.

"I am so thirsty," I mumbled once again.

As I chomped down on another one, that pesky sensation seemed to get worse with each passing second. "Can you ask my doctor if this is normal?" I begged him. This feeling was getting out of control.

My nurse brought me a glass of water, which I also downed in a single gulp. Nothing was working. Oh, and now I really had to pee. Like, *really* had to pee.

What in the world?

The nurse gave it a name. Diabetes insipidus. An unquenchable sensation of thirst caused by the failure of the pituitary gland to produce a critical hormone called vasopressin. While they were up there poking around in my brain, that important little gland got jostled and resulted in a complication that many brain surgery patients know all too well.

To sum it up, having DI means that you're constantly thirsty and you pee nonstop. Upon diagnosis, you assume the role of "worst person to go on a road trip with" and immediately become the girl who carries a water canteen everywhere she goes. In the long list of potential surgery complications, this was one of the ones I failed to take note of while signing off on the procedure.

It hadn't sounded like a big deal at the time, but sitting in my hospital bed and feeling like my insides were turning into dust was a slightly different story. Yikes.

This was, without a doubt, foreshadowing for how the next few months of my life would unfold: Panic googling and middle-of-the-night ER visits. Asking far-too-personal questions in support groups. Crying, so much crying, when I wished things could "just go back" to the way they were before.

Sitting in that hospital bed, I knew that the surgery might be over, but the hardest part, the process of healing, was just beginning.

Here is the truth: It is hard to navigate the darkest valleys of our lives. No one can prepare you for them. The unrelenting pain, the paralyzing fear, the fiery rage, the depths of despair—sometimes spread apart and other times coming for you all at once. There is no way around them. No magic button to make them go away. There is only moving forward. Step by step, bit by bit, you learn how to navigate through the darkness.

EMPOWERED TO OVERCOME

After my brain surgery, there were several months when I relied entirely on the support of others. My community carried me. Home-cooked meals delivered to our doorstep. Prayers from friends across the globe. Constant phone calls and handwritten cards to ensure that I never once lost sight of the love that surrounded me.

For the first time since starting my business, I was forced to rely on the community that I spent so many years building for others. Nearly every day for a month, Rising Tide leaders and small-business buddies took over my social media accounts. They created content for my blog and recorded videos for my Instagram.

During the weeks when I was forced to focus on my health, they made sure that my business would be waiting for me on the other side of recovery.

My community carried me—personally and professionally. They took work off my plate and worries from my mind. They showed up and stepped up. They kept my world moving when I wasn't able to do it myself.

Our culture tells us to feign a false narrative of having it all together—don't tell people if you are lonely, if your business is struggling, or if you are scared or hurting. But the value of our community shines brightest in our moments of struggle.

When we are weak, our community is strong. When we struggle, our community rises up to take the load from our shoulders. Relationships strengthen our resilience. In a way, our connection to others can directly empower us to overcome the adversity we are facing.

The truth about resilience, about that unrelenting grit that keeps us moving forward, is that it is strengthened by our connections to others. Surrounding yourself with encouraging, supportive, and empowering people can truly make all the difference.

But don't just take my word for it. According to the Harvard Graduate School of Education, "When confronted with the fallout of childhood trauma, why do some children adapt and overcome, while others bear lifelong scars that flatten their potential? A growing body of evidence points to one common answer: Every child who winds up doing well has had at least *one stable and committed relationship* with a supportive adult."[1]

One relationship. It's truly that simple. One strong and impactful relationship can be the difference between children who rise above their adversity and those who don't. This applies to all of us as well.

In order to strengthen our resilience, we must be open and willing to tear down those narratives that tell us to go at it alone. We must open our eyes to the outstretched arms all around us. We must be willing to give and to accept help.

We must choose to kick our ego to the curb, set aside our fears of being vulnerable, and let people in. We have to surrender what is picture perfect for what is real. We must embrace what makes us beautifully broken and therefore distinctly human. Then, and only then, can our community come alongside us to carry the heavy load.

DON'T GIVE UP THE SHIP

It was the summer of 1955 when my grandfather, Frank, reported for induction day at the United States Naval Academy. A towering teenager at six foot four, he had gotten in on a congressional third alternate appointment after committing to play football for the navy blue and gold.

This meant that Frank, along with others who were approved admission as second- and third-round picks in order to fill quota, were arriving a few days late. Standing outside the admissions office, he met his future roommate, Jack, upon swearing in. After Plebe Summer, he and Jack would remain roommates for all four years.

Jack was an athletic fellow with an assertive personality who would never back away from a good prank. They shared a sense of humor and a deeply rooted faith. My grandfather knew right away that they were going to be friends.

When you enter the academy, you arrive on campus several weeks before the start of classes. As is tradition, you hug your family goodbye and march—yes, literally march—into the most grueling year of your life as a plebe (a freshman).

Day after day in the hot summer sun you are pushed to the limit and held to the highest standard. Pristine uniforms and shined shoes are required at all formations and inspections. Haircuts are frequent, with lengths never to exceed the collar. Showers are short, and personal time is limited.

You learn how to tie knots, sail boats, and qualify with the .45-caliber pistol and the M1 rifle. *You march.*

There are obstacle courses to run, ropes to climb, and parallel bars to swing from. *You march some more.*

You must tread water for forty minutes while being weighed down by heavy military clothes. *Then you march again.* By the time you are done marching and your head hits the pillow, you are nearly too tired to fall asleep. Plebe Summer is arduous.

Several days before Labor Day, the brigades of upperclassmen arrive. Unfortunately, then it only gets harder. The older midshipmen make it their mission to ensure that all plebes are put to the test. Struggling young plebes must march down the center of the hallways and can only take the long way around—no cutting corners, no shortcuts ever.

At mealtimes during the school year, all four thousand midshipmen are fed together at one sitting. Stainless-steel platters are brought to the tables with large trays full of meat and sides. When the food arrives, the seniors get access first, and they take the choice pieces. Afterward, second classmen and then third classmen have their go. By the time it gets to the plebes, there are only leftovers remaining.

No one goes hungry, but they certainly don't get the best parts of the meal.

Once the plebes get their turn to eat, upperclassmen start grilling them with questions. Hard questions. If you don't know the answer, you respond, "I'll find out, sir." You don't guess. If, God forbid, you answer incorrectly, anticipate a verbal assault from all directions. All of this difficulty is by design.

As a plebe, you are in enemy territory at all times. You are all at the bottom of the totem pole, and it is a steep, strenuous climb to the top. These intentional hardships are a critical rite of passage. Each future officer embarks upon a personal quest to prove that they won't give up, to prove that if push comes to shove, they are willing to lay their life on the line for their country.

My grandfather, in recounting the hardship of that summer, remembers one thing above the rest. No matter how hard it got, he never had to face it alone.

Jack was right there with him when he was running late to class or formation. It was always crunch time. Making sure his shoes were shined, his uniforms were pressed. Picking up the slack when classes ran behind or challenges arose. Jack always had Frank's back, and my grandfather had his.

On the obstacle course, the high platform was my grandfather's greatest challenge, a towering structure with a ledge five feet off the ground. Plebes had to climb their way over the barricade in order to reach the other side. Frank had trouble clearing the high platform, whereas Jack was able to get over easily.

To help my grandfather pass the test, Jack reached out his arm from the top of the platform and pulled him up and over. One outstretched hand and the pair passed the test just in time. It was a triumph through teamwork.

Back and forth they helped each other. Amid the sailing and studying, they held each other accountable and carried the other's load when the weight became too much to bear.

You see, as a plebe you are taught early on to look out for one another. The only way through it is together. You are all in the same boat, figuratively and quite literally.

Every day at noon, midshipmen march together in formation outside of Bancroft Hall. A towering building of stone, it sits at the heart of the academy grounds. They line up in front of the building perfectly before proceeding to lunch.

There is a famous flag that hangs inside Bancroft. It glimmers above a marble staircase leading to Memorial Hall, which honors all USNA grads who died in combat defending the United States. On the flag is a phrase sewn onto the fabric that bears a motto my grandfather has repeated time and time again from when I was young: "Don't Give Up the Ship."

These five words were the dying battle cry of twenty-seven-year-old Captain James Lawrence, captain of the USS *Chesapeake* in the War of 1812. After he was mortally wounded, his heartfelt plea to his crew was to refuse surrender at all costs. Despite his final words, the British overtook the American fleet and the battle was lost.

Months later, the war raged on. Fellow naval officer, Commodore Oliver Hazard Perry, upon hearing of his late friend's passing, named his ship the *Lawrence* and commissioned a flag emblazoned with his friend's final phrase. In battle, Perry set out to finish what his friend could not. Turning his pain into purpose, he used these words to inspire others to bravery.

As he sailed into battle against the British on Lake Erie, Oliver Hazard Perry raised the flag in honor of his comrade. The Americans were victorious, and the phrase "don't give up the ship" has lived on ever since.

It is an anthem to persevere and a reminder that all sailors are in it together until the end. It demands that we stand united in moments when it would be easier for us to abandon ship—and abandon one another.

Plebe year at the Naval Academy is about so much more than strengthening midshipmen physically and mentally. It is about forging friendships in the fire and clarifying the core value of camaraderie in the face of adversity. It is a lesson about the strength of camaraderie and refusing to give up when your buddy is relying on you to move forward.

My grandfather and Jack remained friends for the rest of their lives. They were truly inseparable—spending the school year involved in athletics, helping each other in academics, and spending their summer leave together. This lasted for all four years at the Naval Academy.

Commissioning sent them in different directions, the marine corps for Jack and the air force for Frank, but they always stayed in touch. Several times they reconnected at various duty stations while on leave. After separation from the service, they resumed seeing each other quite often on vacations and at most of the navy football games, until Jack passed away a few years ago.

Fifty-seven years of steadfast friendship. No matter where their careers took them, through seasons of hardship and seasons of prosperity, they would forever remain bonded in the brotherhood of service, dedicated to their country and to each other.

Friendships can be forged in the fire.
Facing challenges together bonds us. Enduring hard seasons side by side unites us. However, so often when we are facing hardship, we withdraw from the world and try to overcome it alone. We become fearful of letting people in. We become afraid to be vulnerable about what we are walking through, and we all suffer for it.

The next time you are facing a particularly difficult season of life, try this instead:

- **Be open with your loved ones about what you are going through.** Don't hustle to hide it. Don't repress your feelings while trying to appear as though you have it all together. Start by being honest. Remember that vulnerability invites more vulnerability. To kick off the conversation, start with: "I trust you and want to confide in you about something that I'm really struggling with. I'm not looking for advice. I just want to be honest with you about what I'm going through."
- **Search for a support group.** There are groups for nearly every human experience, and they can be a powerful place to forge relationships and create connections. Four of the most powerful words in the human language are: you are not alone. Find a group that gets it, and when you make it to the other side of your season of struggle, remember to pay it forward by giving back to the groups that gave so much to you.
- **Ask for help when you need it.** When you are struggling, speak up. We can't expect people to read our minds and know precisely what we need. We also cannot push away help that is offered

to us because of our pride. We must be willing to ask for and accept assistance in our seasons of struggle. There is no shame in needing support.

When we're treading water to the brink of exhaustion and someone reaches out their hand to pluck us from the sea, we need to have the courage to take that hand. There are lifeboats all around us for when we need a break from the battles of life. However, in order to make it through, we need to be willing to accept assistance from a friend.

Friendships can be forged in the fire.

We not only bond face-to-face, but very often, shoulder-to-shoulder, working alongside one another through challenging seasons and personal hardships.

So often we think of relationships as something that stems from seasons of prosperity, but I truly believe that community is strongest in the struggle. It is strengthened by shared experience and is designed to be our safe place to land.

We must be willing to open our hearts to the possibility of doing life with others…not just when we have it all together, but also when the world is falling apart. That is the place where the community shines the brightest. That is the moment when we discover the impact of belonging.

CHAPTER TEN

OVERCOMING COMPARISON

Growing up, we are taught to believe that when we're ready to have a baby, it will just happen. Heck, as a Catholic kid, I worried that looking at a boy the wrong way would accidentally get me pregnant. Mary was a virgin, remember? Those nuns really know how to scare us.

The picture of parenthood is always painted a certain way. Broad, simple brushstrokes on a pristine canvas. When two people are ready for a family, it just happens.

Boom. There are candles, a little Marvin Gaye, and nine months later…an adorable bald baby enters the world. Right?

No one talks about how many people are yearning deeply for a child— waiting to become parents or expand their family, experiencing loss, going through adoption, searching for a surrogate, or battling infertility. No one really talks about the vast routes to parenthood and the pain that often accompanies the journey.

Three years into marriage with an infertility diagnosis resulting from a benign brain tumor, I walked into a clinic with my husband for the first time. There is nothing that says romance quite like a cold sterile hospital room, nitrile gloves, and thousands of dollars in medical bills. Making a baby was nothing like we thought it would be.

I still remember the butterflies I felt in my stomach as I walked into the fertility doctor's office. This was the beginning of our journey. This doctor was going to fix whatever was going wrong with me. Framed diplomas and plaques covered the walls. This doctor was the real deal—and with his help, I was going to join the mom club.

His eyes scanned the documents on his desk. Cluttered white papers from corner to corner: dozens of hormone tests, ultrasound reports, and my brain MRI laid out in the open. His eyes rose to meet mine.

"I don't think it's smart to begin fertility treatment at this time."

His words sent a searing-hot pain straight down into my stomach. With a giant heap of empathy, our fertility endocrinologist went on to explain that my brain tumor would need to be removed or dealt with through radiation or medication before proceeding with a healthy pregnancy.

I nodded stoically. When inside, my mind was screaming, *Wait, what? You mean, we can't even start treatment? We need to wait even longer? You won't help me?*

I was crushed.

This doctor's entire job was to help women get pregnant. All those framed accolades were proof that he was one of the best in the business. Yet, somehow, my body was too broken for him to fix. This was never part of my plan.

None of this was part of my plan.

The two years that followed that first appointment were painful. One by one my friends got pregnant—all in the same pattern: a happy announcement on social media, baby shower invitations in the mail, and a flood of newborn photographs a few months later. Every milestone, every joyous moment, every time I refreshed my feed.

Not a month went by when I wouldn't sneakily take a pregnancy test, get the same negative result, and then bury the evidence deep in our tiny bathroom trash can so that my husband wouldn't know what I had done. I was ashamed to admit that I still had hope—afraid that he would have to share in my latest round of disappointment.

I tried so hard to hide my pain, and yet it only continued to grow. The deeper I tried to bury it, the more violently it would emerge every time it was awakened by someone else's joy.

She just announced her pregnancy. That girl I went to high school with is having twins. Oh, matching family pajamas at Christmas—isn't that lovely!

With each passing month, it became harder and harder to celebrate my friends in their newfound seasons of parenthood. Each pregnancy announcement, every baby shower invitation, was just a reminder of my barrenness.

I was angry with myself. Bitterness replaced my joy. Jealousy consumed me. My lungs inhaled hope and exhaled misery. The endless cycle of comparison and grief was poisoning me slowly from the inside out.

I didn't like the person I was becoming. This was a lesson that I didn't want to have to learn, a painful journey that I never wanted to embark on, and it was going to transform me irrevocably. I could only hope that it would be for the better.

DEFEATING MY NEMESIS

Comparison isn't just the thief of joy—it's the plunderer of purpose, the burglar of belonging. It is a dagger forged in the fires of our deepest fears and insecurities that threatens our very well-being.

We cannot fully benefit from the healing power of community or navigate the world with a deep sense of acceptance when we are constantly struggling with our own enoughness. A joyful life alongside others requires that we shift our tendencies away from negatively comparing ourselves and toward openly celebrating others.

> Comparison isn't just the thief of joy—it's the plunderer of purpose, the burglar of belonging.

Look, I know this isn't easy. I just shared a glimpse into my own struggles with comparison in one of my darkest seasons, and it isn't pretty. I don't like admitting how hard I have struggled with this. However, I know that I'm not alone.

It isn't always big things. Sometimes it's the simplest aspects of daily life that catch you in a comparison trap.

Ready for my realization?

Modern life exacerbates our innate desire to compare and our longing to understand where we fit in the world. We used to compare ourselves to a handful of people in our immediate circle—now it's ten thousand other people on the internet.

On social media, our competitive mindsets can go into overdrive. Scrolling and consuming the story lines of others leads to an amalgamation of accomplishments, heaped into a massive mountain that our minds are incapable of climbing. Like the snowball effect, each win or success in someone else's life gets piled onto the heap of evidence of why you're not measuring up.

What starts as: He has the perfect home. She landed a promotion at work. They have the perfect kids.

Evolves into: Everyone except for me has the perfect home, the perfect kids, career success, and the perfect life.

We consume independent pieces of information, meticulously curated to portray each of our lives in the best light possible and mesh them together into a joy-draining perception of the way things are.

We construct a false narrative of reality and begin to accept it as truth.

In our moments of weakness, we turn the celebrations of others into a weapon against ourselves. A weapon that we create and construct in our own minds. Comparison can quickly become a sword of self-sabotage that leaves us feeling inadequate.

At least, that's how it can feel sometimes…right?

The underlying truth is that social comparison is a hardwired part of the human experience and in its simplest form is an innate act of self-evaluation. In order to understand how we are performing in life, our brain looks to others as a benchmark.

Psychologists commonly categorize social comparison in two ways: upward and downward comparison.

Upward comparison involves comparing ourselves to someone we perceive as better off than we are. Downward comparison involves comparing ourselves to someone we perceive as worse off than we are. Think of it like a swinging pendulum between two different perspectives: "It could always be better" or "It could definitely be worse."[1]

For example, we see someone at work who is getting a promotion or creating their own business and aspire to reach similar heights (upward comparison). We may also look at someone who is struggling in the office and find ourselves feeling pleased that we aren't in their shoes at that moment in time (downward comparison).

Neither upward nor downward comparison is inherently bad. However, our underlying feelings play a significant role in which direction we take and, ultimately, the outcome of how we feel when it is all said and done.

When we have negative emotions, we are much more likely to compare ourselves with people we perceive to be better than us, which in turn further worsens our overall well-being. That endless scrolling, that comparison monster created from the accumulation of everyone else's accomplishments in upward comparison only further exacerbates how we were feeling all along. It affirms our deepest fears and provides us with the proof we were looking for—that we aren't measuring up.

The opposite is true, however, when we set out to make ourselves feel better. When we want to feel good, we're more likely to compare ourselves with people we perceive to be worse off than us, and then, for the most part, our well-being improves...at least for a short while.[2]

Frankly, I'm not a fan of relying on downward comparison to create the illusion of happiness and satisfaction. The pain or struggle of others is not a reason to find joy—even when it illustrates the blessings in our lives. It's just temporary pain relief that we choose over doing the hard work of healing what is broken. We must fight against that.

We deserve to know that we are inherently enough, that we are worthy of love and belonging, without having to compare ourselves to others. And in order to navigate the tendencies that are hardwired within us, we must reframe our mindsets, dig deeper for an empathy-centered truth, and practice gratitude daily.

FLIPPING THE SCRIPT

If you are a chronic comparer, please know that you are not alone. Time and time again, I have fallen back into the same traps of questioning my worth when insecurities crept up. Especially during those six years of marriage leading up to the birth of my firstborn, every pregnancy announcement felt like a dagger in my chest. It was an inescapable pain that was always lurking in the shadows, waiting to rip away my joy and replace it with the belief that my body was failing me.

I was never sure when it would appear: matching pajamas during the holidays, another Mother's Day empty-handed. However, as friends one by one announced their pregnancies, my personal struggle with comparison became a daily battle. One that I had to learn, conscious thought by conscious thought, to fight back against.

One of the most powerful tools in the mindset-shifting toolbox that you've seen me use numerous times in this book (and in my doodles) is the act of cognitive reframing. As a reminder, reframing means taking an existing perception of how things are and changing the narrative in favor of a better outcome. Turning the tables. Flipping the script. Changing the game.

In the case of comparison, I like to think of cognitive reframing as kicking jealousy out of the driver's seat and reclaiming control of the vehicle that is your life. Replacing envy with compassion, empathy, and joy.

So, how does it work? I'll show you. Let's take a look at some examples of upward comparisons that we may come across in our daily lives and examine how to shift away from negative perceptions and toward a positive view of our experience.

	FROM THIS	**TO THAT**
Career Success	She is so much more successful than I am—her business is booming and I can't even get mine off the ground. I am a failure.	Wow! She is on fire! Seeing her achieve that level of success shows me the magnitude of what is possible. I can do it too.
Family Life	She has three beautiful kids before thirty, and I'm nowhere near that season of life. My priority is my career. I must be falling behind and missing out.	I'm grateful that we all have the freedom to pursue different callings. There is no single timeline or set of milestones that determine success. She deserves happiness and so do I.
Physical Health	She has the perfect body, and when she parades it around on social media, it makes me feel unworthy. I will never look like her.	It's amazing to see another woman comfortable in her own skin. I deserve to feel that confident and love myself fully.

This technique is all about shifting our mindset away from comparison and toward a celebration of others. It means accepting that other people are not our enemy. It means welcoming the accomplishments of others rather than using those achievements as proof of your unworthiness.

We have a choice when we see others climbing higher, when they are reaching goals that none of us thought were possible. We can cheer them on or we can tear them down.

If we choose to tear them down, if we discount their accomplishments and judge their successes, if we make it harder for others to succeed, then we all lose. That failure is shared by the collective because we all remain trapped together beneath that impenetrable ceiling.

If we choose to cheer others on, if we make an effort to raise their voices and fan the flames of their success, then we are all the better for it. When someone else wins, we all win. When someone else wins, it affirms that it is possible for all of us.

When someone else finds happiness, achieves greatness, it doesn't take away from your ability to do the same. You can celebrate the accomplishments of others without feeling diminished by their prosperity.

Moving past mindsets of comparison to truly embrace, celebrate, and empower one another requires so much more from us than mental gymnastics. It requires taking action. Once you've mastered this mindset and have reached a season in life when you are ready to pour back into others, do it.

When we become the success stories that we once compared ourselves to, we have a responsibility to make it easier for the ones who come after us. We must use our power to empower others—ensuring that we are not a one-hit wonder, but rather the start of a shift in the status quo. We may have to fight our internal narratives to do it, but it is up to us to turn the tide.

We must become the empowering and affirming voices that we wish we had when we were in the arena. The comparison of our past can become the camaraderie of our future. The choice is ours.

WE ARE ICEBERGS

It all began with a question. "If I don't like the way I look in my images, you can make me skinnier, right? You can fix my arms, my waistline?"

The bride looked at me across the table with a completely serious stare. This was 2009—long before filters or apps that made it easy to change your appearance at the drop of a hat. Instagram wouldn't be created for another year.

I know it might seem like a common question today. However, this wasn't the case back then. It was jarring.

This was the first time in my career as a professional wedding photographer that I was being asked to do this. I froze. Sitting across from this bride-to-be, I was suddenly faced with an issue much greater than I was ready to understand.

For me, the question was not whether I could manipulate her images to make her resemble her bridal magazine covers—airbrushed, liquified, and perfected in Photoshop—but whether I should.

So I sat there staring back at this gorgeous young woman as my own insecurities came bubbling to the surface.

Shoot. If someone "like her" wasn't happy with her body, how could anyone "like me" be satisfied with the way I looked? I was even further from her definition of beautiful. My waistline was curvier, and I had dozens of scars on my arms and stretch marks on my hips. I tried not to take it personally, but her question made me feel like crap.

My stomach turned. My cheeks felt hot. Make no mistake—at nineteen years old and paying my way through college, I needed the money. I really needed to book this wedding.

However, I just couldn't give her the answer that she wanted. I couldn't say yes.

So she booked another photographer.

I'm not going to lie to you—it sucked. To make matters worse, year after year the requests became more frequent, and the practice of editing our appearances and, along with them, our lives became more and more commonplace.

My realization, beyond the fact that the world was desperately in need of a body positivity and inclusivity movement, was this:

The images we consume, the content all around us, only tells half the story.

The other half gets buried behind the painstakingly curated images and delicately crafted highlight reels that we see in our daily scroll. The other half gets airbrushed out or hidden from the algorithms that popularize what the world deems to be beautiful. The other half is too hard to write into words or express on the internet.

> **The images we consume, the content all around us, only tells half the story.**

The other half, the most vulnerable and honest half of our lives gets left behind.

It's no one single person's fault.

We are all human. Our insecurities are so deep, our past trauma so vast and wide, that sometimes we do whatever we can to hide it. We are imperfect beings doing the best that we can and struggling with things in our hearts that the rest of the world will never see. None of us is exempt from it.

When we struggle, we're told "Chin up, buttercup. Don't let them see you cry. Put your best foot forward and keep pressing on."

So we do. We tidy up our hearts as if the mess within us is too much for others to bear, and we tuck away our grief in the deepest corner of our beings. We know that there is so much more beneath the surface, there is so much depth to our experiences that the world will never truly witness. We are imperfect beings doing the best we can in a broken world...and often wading through the waters of shame that threaten to swallow us whole.

We are little icebergs—the beauty and joy glimmering just above the water, with so much more that lies beneath the surface. Dynamic and wondrous, the complexity of our lives cannot be fully understood in a single image or a caption.

None of what I just said is new to any of us. We know that there is so much more to our stories than what we share online or in community settings. However, when we turn our gaze to others, we are so quick to forget.

With phones in hand and the internet at our fingertips, we take the half-truths and highlight reels and stitch them together into a reality that feels far superior to our own. We construct a picture of the world from the best parts of other people's stories and wonder why our lives feel so much messier.

In order to break through that, in order to build deep and lasting bonds with others, we must dig deeper. We must accept that things on the surface are rarely indicative of how things truly are.

I'm an iceberg. You're an iceberg. Everyone in the world is a freaking iceberg.

And if we continue barreling through life without acknowledging that there is so much more to others beneath the surface, we're going to crash. If we keep comparing and comparing and comparing, we're going to sink like the *Titanic* and spend the rest of our lives wondering if there really was enough room for Jack to survive on the floating door with Rose after all.

So how do we go deep in a shallow world? How do we get past the highlight reels and curated feeds? How do we stop comparing and start truly loving one another?

One word: empathy.

Empathy is mirror neurons firing on all cylinders. Our brains are equipped with emotional intelligence and wired to imagine what it would feel like to experience the world from someone else's situation. It's a critical component of human connection.

Empathy is the ability to put yourself in someone else's shoes, and in the case of comparison in the digital age, to acknowledge that there is so much more than what meets the eye. It means occasionally reading between the lines and reminding ourselves daily that every person we meet is fighting a tough battle.

Accessing empathy enables us to eradicate thoughts that put the lives of others on a pedestal and replace them with deeply held compassion, kindness, and respect for the challenges they have faced to get to where they are today.

The mother with three beautiful kids also has two angel babies in heaven. That entrepreneur who just went full time was actually laid off by a boss who told her that she would never make anything of herself. The person you compare yourself to on social media has a painful past and a trunk full of trauma that never makes its way onto their Instagram feed.

Human beings are not highlight reels.

Consciously seeking empathy-centered truth means kicking any notions of perfection to the curb and training your brain to catch half-truths before they become the full picture.

In the battle against comparison, empathy is the key.

> **Human beings are not highlight reels.**

GROUNDED IN GRATITUDE

Something tells me that at the end of our lives, we won't look back and wish that we had spent more time comparing ourselves to other people on the internet. Something tells me that we won't long for the hours we wasted counting all the reasons we didn't measure up.

Something tells me that we're going to wish that we had loved ourselves and others just a little bit more…that we had put down the phone and lifted our eyes to see the beauty that surrounded us. Something tells me that we will wonder why we couldn't see it then—all those reasons to be grateful, all those beautiful relationships we so often took for granted.

A grateful heart that celebrates the successes of others is a weapon in the war of comparison. When we're grateful, we're not fearful. And when we're not fearful, we're able to concentrate on what is good in our lives and share that spirit of abundance with others.

Whenever I talk about gratitude, I know that half of the room immediately thinks this bit of advice doesn't apply to them. Perhaps they have heard it time and time again. Perhaps they think it's too fluffy, too abstract, to truly make a meaningful difference in their lives.

Here's where the science comes in. Intentional gratitude changes levels of serotonin and dopamine in the brain. Like a natural dose of Prozac, practicing conscious thankfulness changes our neurochemistry.[3]

When you start comparing your life to someone else's, count the things in your day that are truly special. Take note of the people, experiences, and things that you so often take for granted.

Another tip for chronic comparers like me—start each day with a gratitude activity. Rather than reaching for your phone, reach for a journal. Comparison isn't going away when we put our phones down. However, we can choose to reach for the things that lead us back to ourselves. In that journal, write down three things that you are thankful for that day and spend a few moments reflecting on what you cherish most in your life.

AN END TO THE WAITING

Our season of waiting for fertility treatment ended when we finally evicted my benign brain tumor from its residence in my head. As you've read, it's a much longer story than that—but we'll keep going.

At my post-op appointment, my neurosurgery and endocrine team told us that we could begin trying for a baby six months after surgery.

So exactly six months and two days after the day that I was wheeled into the OR for brain surgery, we walked into our new fertility clinic in San Francisco.

Can you tell that we were just the tiniest bit eager to get started?

A new doctor with an optimistic outlook on our chances assured us that there was hope. Sitting in her office was far different from our experience years before. She was warm and empathetic. I felt seen and heard for the first time on our infertility journey.

The following week we began treatment.

We moved from pills to injections, appointment after appointment, prayer after prayer, until a few months later we received the news that we had been fighting for—it worked. I got a positive test after all those years of yearning.

It was nothing short of a miracle.

I find it difficult to describe the moment we first saw our son on an ultrasound. Simultaneous waves of joy and worry washed over me.

The flutter of our baby's heartbeat was the music that my ears had waited to hear for so long. Those independent notes filled the room in a resounding symphony of redemption. A beautiful new life, nestled in the womb of a woman who never thought she would get the chance to have a baby.

However, the joy of that moment also brought about a new set of fears. There were many, as any pregnant mama can attest to, but the biggest one for me was around sharing the news with the world.

I was terrified to publicly share that I was pregnant.

I kept feeling as though this were all a dream—like after years of waiting, this outcome was far too good to be true. I worried that when we finally shared our happy news with the world, all of this would be ripped away. It felt like everything would come crashing down. Our happiness would just disintegrate through our fingertips, and we would spiral even deeper into a grief that we would never recover from.

And what about all the other women still waiting for their miracle? What about them?

My heart ached. Truly ached. A mixture of guilt and grief that I never could have anticipated. Why not them? What had we done to deserve this blessing? My anger for my friends who were still at war with infertility raged within me.

I had never been on this side of the journey to parenthood, and in all those years, I never actually considered what it would be like to have an announcement of our own to share.

Was this how my friends had felt all those years? Afraid to tell me their happy news? Did they worry about sending out baby shower invitations and struggle to find the right words to say? I wondered.

Did they too struggle to celebrate the joy of this season? Did they fear for this little life every second of every day? I also wondered.

In the complexity of that moment, I was reminded that there is so much more to our stories than what meets the eye.

Even in our victories against the darkest moments of our lives exists a complex layering of the trauma we've traversed to get there. Prosperity and pain can coexist. Grief can intertwine with joy. Worry can weave together with hope in the tapestry of our mind.

No one's experience can be summed up in a single snapshot. No one's journey can be communicated in a few dozen characters. This is what it means to be human.

We waited well into the second trimester to share the news, and when we did, something surprising happened. Yes, our friends were happy for us…but the women who cheered the loudest, the ones who celebrated my success as if it were their own, were the women in my infertility support groups.

I've never experienced such a rallying cry of celebration in my entire life. The most enthusiastic voices came from friends who were still in the battle, the ones still fighting for their miracle moment, who chose to love me amid their own suffering.

If it can happen for her, it can happen for me.

Their outcries of support filled the silence where fear and doubt danced around in my mind. They showed me, through their solidarity and compassion, that we must choose to celebrate others not only when it is easy, but most important, when it is hard.

It was a lesson that I failed to understand so many years before…and through their selfless solidarity, it became a learning that I carry with me to this day.

CHAPTER ELEVEN

FINDING YOUR PEOPLE

Growing up in Annapolis, you see the rowers zipping down the Severn River nearly every morning. They cut through the water like magic—racing up and back, up and back—until it's time to return to the boathouse.

I used to sit by the water and watch them, knowing that when the time was right, I was going to join a team.

At fifteen, I signed myself up for the local rowing club.

My childhood dream was finally coming true! *Watch out, world…*

Across the river that same week, a teenage boy was also registered for rowing—by his mother (completely without his knowledge). Her hope was that rowing would finally get him off the couch, away from his video games, and outside into nature. You can imagine that he was less than thrilled when he found out.

On my first day at the boathouse, I spotted him.

Just shy of six feet, with long, shaggy hair, he was standing beside the towering rack of boats, waiting for practice to begin. I nervously walked up and introduced myself in the most cringeworthy way possible.

"Hey! I'm Natalie," I said with a wave.

"Hi, I'm Hugh," he mumbled.

"Who?" I asked, completely unsure of what he had just said. It sounded a heck of a lot like the word "who," but I had never met anyone with that name before.

"H-U-G-H," he said a bit louder, trying to enunciate his name. I could tell this wasn't the first time he had to do that.

Shaking my head, I responded, "Um, did you just say *whooooo*? I'm sorry, I…"

"Huey," he said kindly. "Just call me Huey."

I laughed.

Yikes, I was bad at this…like, really, really bad at this. I could feel my cheeks turning a familiar shade of red.

"Oh, Huey…That's a cool name. Well, it's really nice to meet you."

Our uncomfortable introduction was swiftly interrupted by the roaring voice of our Russian rowing coach, Veetus, who told us to take a dozen laps around the field before we were ready to rig our first boat. Huey and I took off jogging together, side by side.

We spent that first day at practice partnered up through every exercise and lesson that Veetus threw our way. Neither of us had any idea what we were doing. Likewise, neither of us joined the rowing team expecting to meet our best friend.

Sometimes we cannot quite envision how our lives will change when we disrupt our daily routine to try something new. Sometimes our paths cross with others in the community and our world is never quite the same again.

In setting out to find new passions or breaking free from the patterns of the past, we create room for new relationships to take root. We set out to find a hobby, a cause worth fighting for, a way to connect with nature—and we end up gaining so much more.

Getting out of our comfort zone and switching up our routines can transform our lives. Leaning into community can change everything.

When we are young, the groups that we belong to are primarily those that we were born or adopted into. Our family is, after all, the first community that many of us are a part of. As we grow older, we quickly discover that we are capable of choosing our own connections.

With time, our world view expands beyond what was once familiar. Friendships are formed based on shared interests, experiences, and values. We get involved in causes that we are passionate about or join clubs that bring us joy. We try new things, take up new hobbies.

We finally get the chance to row on the river like we had dreamed of doing since childhood…or we get kicked off the couch against our will and take up rowing all the same.

We also experience the challenges that come with community—rejection, heartbreak, and loss. As adults, we often find ourselves searching for relationships that feel like family, to discover that sense of belonging once again.

However, finding friends as an adult can be difficult. It can be hard to find people you connect with and who accept you for who you truly are. Knowing where to start and where to look for those opportunities to connect can make all the difference.

Start with yourself.

Before you can find community with others, you must first find community within yourself. Embracing who you are and learning to love yourself opens the gateway for meaningful relationships with others.

When you step into your search for community unsure of who you are and weighed down by insecurities, you're more likely to change yourself to fit in rather than seeking a place where you are accepted for who you truly are.

Think of it like this: You are like coffee. If someone wants to water you down with creamer and sweeten you up with sugar, then you might not be the right friend for them, and that's okay. You don't need to change yourself to be liked, and knowing that at the start of your quest to find community is important.

Searching for true belonging means that we must know and love ourselves first. It is from a place of self-confidence that we step forward boldly into finding a community where we truly belong.

Start right where you are.

You don't need to look far to find meaningful ways to engage in community. The spaces where we live, work, exercise, and worship are already rich in opportunities to connect with others. Begin with a list of the spaces and groups that you are already a part of and analyze whether you are truly engaging in the opportunities that already exist.

Oftentimes, I find that people are surrounded by communities; however, they aren't truly connected to them.

Sometimes this is due to the fear of rejection or the misperception that wading in the shallow end of relationships is enough to fill our cup. Sometimes it is caused by a misalignment between what we truly need and where we are spending our time. Sometimes it is because we have outgrown the spaces where we once belonged, and it is time to stretch our wings.

Communities like friendships can come into our lives for a season. They can grow and change just as we do. They can serve us well and then no longer be what we need. When you start by looking right where you are, you can learn a lot about what is working and what is not.

Remember, it is okay to admit that the communities you are a part of are not serving you in this season. It is also okay to recommit and lean in deeper to the places where you see the potential for meaningful relationships.

From here, we can set out to find our community. I have a simple three-step framework to help you get there, and then we can talk about what to do once you've found a good opportunity to engage.

It starts with understanding what you are looking for.

1. Identify the type of community you need.

Before you head to a search engine and stare at a blank cursor, wondering where to find a community in which you'll belong, you must understand the type of community that best fits this season of your life.

Different types of communities serve different purposes. There are communities centered around taking action, a common passion, shared life experiences, a specific place, or profession. There are communities that meet in-person and others that meet online. There are weekly gatherings and annual conventions.

Below we dive into five taxonomies that house an infinite list of groups and subgroups. It is important to note that this is far from exhaustive. However, it is a broad enough framework to help you think through the places where you can connect with others so that you can truly find your people.

1. **Action:** Action-oriented communities are centered around an external problem that needs solving. These groups are

made up of people trying to bring about positive change in areas that matter deeply to them.

Think of something that you would like to see change in the world or your hometown, then look for a group of others who are actively trying to accomplish that.

Examples of action-oriented communities include volunteer opportunities, grassroots movements, political parties/ action groups, fundraising efforts, environmental groups, and social-justice organizations. Many charities have opportunities to volunteer, which can lead to long-term community-led opportunities to serve and make a positive impact.

2. **Passion:** These communities unite around a mutual interest or shared passion. Passion communities can be built upon something broad like a love of cooking or dive deep into something niche like macrame artistry or geocaching. There are passion communities for nearly every obscure hobby and interest imaginable.

Think of something you like to do or learn about. It can be a childhood interest you want to reexplore as an adult, a sport you would like to try, or a random fact that you want to learn more about. There is likely a group that actively discusses or meets around that shared passion.

Examples of passion communities often take the shape of clubs and conventions on nearly any topic you can imagine. Some are massive, like Comic-Con, while others are small, like a local kickball league or bird-watching group.

3. **Shared experience:** These communities center around a shared lived experience that is unique to the group, where members can connect on what they are going through or have walked through. These groups often center around solidarity or the pursuit of healing and can be community-led or organized by a professional. Sometimes they are designed to be lifelong, whereas other times the goal is to reach a point where you can move into a different community or leave altogether.

One of the most common examples of groups centered around a shared life experience are support groups designed to help people navigating an unfamiliar circumstance, illness, addiction, loss, or a difficult season. There are groups for breast cancer survivors, triplet moms, and alcoholics in recovery—all designed to support the members by connecting them with others who have endured a similar experience.

Within Rising Tide we have two shared-experience groups—our chapter for creatives with chronic illness and our chapter for business owners who are part of a military family. Members of both groups feel safe sharing and getting advice from fellow business owners who are enduring similar life experiences because they share a unique perspective (like the challenges of building a business with a chronic illness; the uncertainty of planting roots and opening your business when the military is likely to move you without notice).

Being part of infertility communities has been particularly helpful for me during my seasons of treatment. Having a safe space to ask questions, share frustrations, and find people who truly understand can make all the difference.

Shared-experience communities can serve a powerful purpose in new or challenging seasons in our lives.

4. **Proximity:** Communities based on proximity are built around a shared place or space that all members are connected to. Oftentimes proximity is an additional filter through which communities are niched down. However, it can be a stand-alone reason to gather.

   When my husband and I moved to San Francisco, we had a group of friends from Maryland that met up frequently. We were all West Coast transplants, and we appreciated being around fellow Marylanders every once in a while. (It's nice to not be judged for carrying Old Bay with you everywhere—okay?)

   Examples of proximity-based communities include local gatherings, festivals, and geographically based hobbies that are deeply connected to a specific place. They can be specific to local culture or an annual tradition. They can also center around the nostalgia of a different place that connects all members in a new one (like expatriates that gather in foreign countries or my Maryland friend group meeting up in San Francisco).

5. **Professional:** These communities unify around a shared profession or set of skills that you desire to learn in the advancement of your career or business. Members often share

knowledge with one another or engage in workshops that give them access to critical information.

Examples of professional communities include business networking groups, unions, guilds, and skill-building organizations. Some are free to join, while others cost a fee to attend. Each serves to help you unite with others who share similar career goals, aspirations, or experiences.

Not all communities will fit neatly in one of the boxes above. Some communities will take elements from different types and merge them to be more niche or to serve the needs of its members more deeply.

For example, Rising Tide local chapters are a cross between a professional and a proximity community. They are reserved for small-business owners operating within a certain geographic area and meet in person once a month. They are based in specific cities and serve to help small-business owners rise together, lifting the local economy.

2. Determine whether you want to connect online, offline, or both.

The second step to finding your community is to determine whether you are looking for online or offline opportunities to connect. There is no right or wrong answer here. Both can offer incredibly meaningful avenues to get to know others and engage in community.

How do you determine which is best for you?

- Understand your availability, ability, and limitations. Is it possible for you to attend in-person gatherings? Are you in a season of life or under certain constraints that make one option better than the other?

- Discern your preference. Do you prefer getting to know people in person or online? Where do you feel that you can be most yourself?

Starting with these simple questions can narrow down the scope of search that you'll embark upon in step three. Additionally, know that there are ways to engage in every single type of community that we talked about: in person, online, or even in a hybrid model.

One of the most transformative things to come out of the coronavirus pandemic was the movement of offline communities into the online world. Physical distancing forced organizers to leverage technology, thereby transforming our ability to connect in significant ways.

Remember that there is immense value in online community that should not be disregarded in our race to return to a pre-pandemic world. Online communities provide additional access to people who cannot or prefer not to meet in person. They enable a more inclusive structure for facilitating meaningful dialogue and relationships.

3. Find your group.

We've talked about starting where you are and doing a quick assessment of your existing opportunities to engage. Then we broke down the different types of communities that exist and how you can think about the role of each on your life and dove into whether online or offline connection is the right path for you. Our final step is to go out and find the exact community that you're looking for so that you can begin getting involved, connecting with others, and building relationships.

Starting the search for your ideal community doesn't have to be overwhelming.

You can pop online or phone a friend. You can look up hashtags and search geolocations on social media, browse bulletin boards in coffee shops, and chat with neighbors from your front porch. You can look at products that you use, places where you exercise, or thought leaders that you follow.

You can also directly search on platforms that facilitate in-person and online groups. There are several, and they are packed with opportunities to get connected.

Some of the most common community platforms include:

- Eventbrite
- Facebook
- Instagram
- Meetup
- Reddit

If you're looking to get out and meet people in person, start with Eventbrite or Meetup. You can search by category or by city and RSVP for gatherings happening in your local area. I guarantee that you'll be surprised by the number of events happening all around you on a daily basis…most of them that you've never heard of.

If you need support or have an interest area that you want to learn more about, search on Facebook or Instagram. On Facebook, start by searching for groups. On Instagram, you can browse accounts, geolocations, and hashtags to narrow in on relevant groups to engage with.

Have an obscure topic that you love learning about or contributing to conversation online? There is a subreddit for that. With more than 430 million monthly active users worldwide, Reddit is a platform that facilitates forums on nearly every subject imaginable.[1] You can also learn about other communities through Reddit forums, as it serves as a central hub of information and is community-led.

Additionally, you can always take to a search engine and specifically look for groups or gatherings near you that align with your interests. It doesn't matter how obscure your interest is, there is almost always a community that unites around that thing, idea, or place.

Hop on to Google and type "your area of interest here community." It might take a little digging, but you'll be surprised by how much you find.

OVERCOMING THE FIRST-TIME PHOBIA

Once you find a group that you want to engage with, it is natural to feel nervous to take the next step. I get it. I get anxious when attending new meet-ups or joining new groups.

For someone writing a book about community, it is embarrassing to admit that on more than one occasion, I have driven to a gathering, sat in my car nervously, and failed to muster the confidence to walk in the front door. I have RSVP'd yes and chickened out at the last minute.

Battling with social anxiety is something I have dealt with since I was a kid. Honestly, I think it is part of what makes me good at what I do.

I am empathetic to the fears that many people feel once they have found a community that they truly want to be a part of. There are simple techniques that make it easier to bridge the gap between where you are and where you want to be in relationships with others.

Here are my tried-and-true techniques for breaking through the fear of first-time attendance and cultivating a stronger connection with members of your newly found community.

- **Create a confidence-boosting ritual.** Before attending the event online or in person, create a ritual that helps you to feel your best. For in-person gatherings, I choose an outfit that I feel confident in, leave thirty minutes early to avoid anxiety around traffic and parking, and turn on a pump-up playlist. For online meet-ups, I give myself extra time to make a cup of coffee so that I have something to sip. You can set yourself up for success by taking time to think through how you want to feel when you show up to your community event and cultivating a pre-event experience that fosters that.

- **Eliminate negative self-talk.** Start by identifying the negative narratives that serve as your internal talk track around engaging in community and replace them with positive affirmations. Speak to yourself optimistically and list out truths about your best qualities and inherent worthiness. Changing your mindset can have a powerful impact on how you carry yourself in conversations and the nuanced body language that others pick up on in the room.

- **Bring a friend.** Sometimes having one person attend with you that you are familiar with can be the difference between hiding in the parking lot and giving it your all. Ask a friend if they will event swap with you. You attend an event with them, and they can attend an event with you. You might even discover something new that you love through their interests. It can be a powerful win-win.

- **Ask good questions.** Show genuine interest in others and seek to first get to know them better. Growing up, when I would feel awkward or shy, my mom always used to tell me, "Just ask good questions. People find it easiest to talk about themselves." As silly as that sounds, she was right. You can learn a lot about a person by asking them to tell you more about what they love and what they are passionate about. It also opens the gateway for them to reciprocate.

- **Repeat their name.** Being able to call someone by name and use it with intentional care throughout your conversation increases levels of trust. It says, *I see you and you matter to me.* Your name is also one of the first words that you learn as an infant, and hearing your own name triggers greater brain activation than when you hear the name of another person.[2]

  Dale Carnegie championed this idea in his book *How to Win Friends and Influence People.* Carnegie said, "A person's name is to him or her the sweetest and most important sound in any language." He certainly was right.[3]

  In the case of meeting my husband, I may have stumbled to get his name right...but I didn't quit until I did. I believe that getting someone's name right matters too.

- **Start with what you have in common.** Have you ever seen a five-year-old walk right up to another five-year-old and say, "I like your blue crayon. I have one too. Want to be my friend?" One minute later they will be running around the playground together as if they have known each other their entire lives.

  Children are always looking for ways to connect on the simplest of things they share—a favorite color, a love of jump rope, a shared pack of cookies in a lunchbox. There is immediate trust upon learning that they share something in common…regardless of how small or insignificant. When you are unsure of where to begin, start with what you have in common with others. Shared interests, passions, and values are a bridge to connection.

Building a foundation with someone on what you share sets the stage so that you can also celebrate what makes you different.

Common ground can give us the footing that we need to cultivate empathy and connection. These initial threads of understanding enable us to dig deeper into the hard work of building lasting relationships and tackling the tough stuff together.

- **Ask for a way to stay connected.** When you hit it off with someone that you enjoyed connecting with or if you want to get more involved in the group, ask for ways to stay connected. You can take the conversation to other platforms or set up a one-on-one with the organizer to learn more. It is important to express interest and take the next step when you find a potential friend or community that you want to stay involved with.

Above all else, as you step into finding your community, remember that others are on a similar journey too. No one is exempt from this quest, and no human being, regardless of how it appears on the outside, has everything figured out.

We are all doing our best to connect. We are all working to overcome our fears. Sometimes the bravest thing we can do is get the courage to leave our parked car and walk through the front door. Sometimes it's introducing yourself to someone new. Sometimes it's getting the courage to push through an awkward introduction.

However, if we face our fears and step into the unknown, there is a good chance that meaningful relationships will be there to meet us on the other side.

It's worth it, friend. I promise you. Take that next step and go out to find your people.

CHAPTER TWELVE

COMMUNITY BUILDING 101

What happens when you set out to find your community and then you discover that it doesn't exist? Or what if you feel deeply called to create something of your own because you have a vision for what a better community could look like? When you can't find it, build it.

There is no rule that says you have to wait for someone else to create the thing that you wish existed. Perhaps you are the leader that you've been waiting for all along.

Community builders come in all shapes and sizes—from a corporate CEO striving to create a stronger company culture to parents seeking to start traditions that instill a deep sense of belonging within their families. Many community cultivators stumble into their leadership roles simply because they care deeply about a group of people or solving a set of problems.

As a small-business owner, my experience with community building began by longing for connection in the competitive entrepreneurial landscape and fighting to find others who believed in the power of partnership.

When I couldn't find the community I was looking for, I decided to create it.

When I set out to become a wedding photographer, I never thought that it would lead into a career in community building. At the beginning, I had no idea what I was doing...and sometimes it showed. Starting Rising Tide was a crash course in community organizing that involved leading imperfectly and stumbling my way through nurturing a rapidly growing group. All the mistakes you can make in starting a community—I've probably made them.

This chapter on community building isn't a theoretical account of how to implement someone else's prescribed best practices. It's a tried-and-true explanation of what worked and what didn't. It's a combination of mistakes made and lessons learned.

So, whether you're creating a company or cultivating a community, growing a team or raising a family, there are several key methods to building a sense of belonging within your group. These are approaches that enabled us to grow Rising Tide from an idea at a dinner table to a thriving community of tens of thousands around the world.

This chapter is about equipping you with everything you need to create your community, lead it well, and inspire others to join you.

ALWAYS START WITH ONE

No community worth being a part of started overnight. Beneath every thriving success story are years of consistent work and relationship building. Showing up countless times before others took notice. Pushing past doubts, fears, and criticism to bring something powerful to the world.

How did Serena Williams learn to play tennis? One swing at a time. Over and over again—when the world was watching and when it was not—Serena showed up, leaving her blood, sweat, and tears on the court every day for decades before she became one of the greatest athletes of all time.

How did Sara Blakely build a business empire with Spanx? One day of hard work after another. On days when no one took her seriously, in boardrooms when others discounted her ideas, Sara showed up, fighting for her seat at the table until she was able to help other women to build businesses of their own.

How did any movement begin to change our world for the better? From Black Lives Matter to Pride to Me Too, our present reality is shaped by the brave actions of individual people. One march and one protest at a time. From one brave leader resisting the way things are, calling out the injustices around them, and demanding better. One voice has the ability to become thousands. One action has the power to change our world.

Communities are built one person at a time.

One conversation, one moment of connection, strung together across time and space over and over again. There is no *POOF* moment of instantaneous creation where a large community comes into existence.

It starts with one. It always starts with one. As a world, we glorify the end result and so often fail to honor the hard-fought journey.

Building authentic and meaningful community is not about racing to the finish line but rather starting small and with intention. One invitation, one conversation, one relationship, one gathering—and then another and another until a sense of belonging is born.

So often we feel rushed to grow our groups and improve our

relationships at scale. It can sometimes feel like you're not doing enough or that community growth is not unfolding as quickly as you had hoped. Be patient and commit to doing the work.

Every month, when our Rising Tide leaders prepare for their local meet-ups, I like to remind them of one thing. Whether one member attends or a group of one hundred gathers, every single person matters. Their role is not to impress the one hundred, but to serve the one.

There is power in showing up for that one person. Countless local chapters have started with one leader and a passionate member sitting together at a table. Just two human beings talking about the impact of fighting for camaraderie amid our culture of competition.

A community leader's job isn't to work tirelessly to build the biggest group in town, but rather to cultivate a space where each individual person who walks through the door feels welcome to pull up a seat and is empowered to share their story.

Cultivating connection in the one-to-one supports community as it scales to many.

It is not about growth. It is about impact. Digging deep is more important than going far and wide. There is no shortcut to the finish line. Cultivating belonging is very hard work, yet it's some of the most rewarding and impactful work we can do.

YOUR FIRST STEPS

If you want to nurture a sense of belonging and keep people engaged in the long run, there are specific techniques that help to grow that spirit from the ground up. Many of these will sound familiar. You see them in your local neighborhood, school, and wellness or faith communities.

They are tenets that shape the way humans interact and have for thousands of years.

The key tenets of a strong community are:

- Mission, vision, and values
- Strong leadership
- Shared experiences

Let's explore these tenets and the ways that you can use them to build the foundation for belonging as you create your community.

1. Define your mission, vision, and values.

All strong communities have a clear mission, vision, and values shared by its leaders and members. These tenets give the community structure and purpose. They communicate who the community is for and what it is striving to achieve.

Imagine a community like a giant caravan of independent cars headed on a road trip to a sought-after destination. All the vehicles in the caravan are separate; however, they are connected by something greater.

On the road trip of life, our mission tells us why we are driving. Our vision paints a picture of the final destination. Our core values shape how we intend to get there.

Building a community around a shared mission, vision, and values enables all members to feel like a part of the team. We are stronger when we are connecting from a foundation of purpose and are all in alignment on the intention for the group.

Create your mission statement.

At its core, a mission statement explains what you do and who you do it for. It should unite and motivate your members to take action. It should also help to define your goals, initiatives, and campaigns.

When creating your mission statement, try filling in the following sentence.

[Community name] is on a mission to [do an action] for [a group of people.]

You can build your mission statement up from there. However, I've found that to be a solid place to start.

For example, Rising Tide's mission is to educate and empower small-business owners to rise together in the spirit of community over competition. We list out what we do (education and empowerment) and who we do it for (small-business owners). We also include a nod to our foundational purpose (helping people rise together in the spirit of community over competition).

A strong mission statement should be clear, concise, and motivational.

Create your vision statement.

A vision statement paints a picture of a world where your mission has been achieved. It gives the community direction and should have an element of aspiration to cast the vision for what a better world could look like.

[Community name] envisions a world where [your mission achieved.]

Think about where you would like to see your community, family, or organization in ten years. Cast your vision from that place. Envision what your world will look like once your mission has been achieved.

Define your core values.

Core values are the foundational beliefs of a community. When shared by the group, they create a feeling of safety and enable people to navigate spaces understanding what to expect from other members of the group.

When things are good, they unite us in a collective rallying cry that drives us toward our mission. When things are hard, they are the guide rails for difficult conversations and a north star while disagreeing well.

Core values reach out a hand and say: *Hey! This is who we are and what we believe in. Our community lives by these beliefs, and we will fight to defend them. If our core values resonate, come on in. You belong here.*

For example, with Rising Tide, we use our core values to create community guidelines that dictate how we expect members to treat one another online and in person. We named these principles our Lifts All Boats Policy. These community rules were built upon the simple premise that we are not here to tear each other down, but rather to lift one another up.

What does it mean to lift all boats? Our community's goal is to provide support, education, and guidance to creative entrepreneurs as they build a business they love. We believe in inclusivity, being better together, and empowerment through education.

We encourage members to ask questions, give advice, dive further into the monthly business topics, encourage each other, support creative colleagues, and seek constructive feedback. We don't shy away from hard, healthy, and robust conversations. We believe that it's important to talk about hard topics and to have these discussions with respect and consideration.

We also draw a hard line with anything that goes against our core values. We don't allow posts that are inherently negative or posted only to cause harm. Our community is not a space to bash clients, other members, or industry peers. It is not a group for gossip or bringing others down.

Any bullying, harassment, or derogatory language will earn you a one-way ticket out of the group, and we have a zero-tolerance policy for discrimination and bigotry. Anyone who attacks or belittles a member or a group of people based on race, gender identity, color, religion, age, nationality, physical or mental disability, marital status, ancestry, veteran status, ethnicity, or sexual orientation is immediately removed. No second chances given.

Core values must be shared publicly and rules stated clearly. For example, guidelines and values for Rising Tide are available on our website and summarized in our Facebook group's description.

So how do you determine your core values? The path is easier than you think.

1. **Choose your stakeholders.** Whose input is critical to define the core values of the community? Think about members or leaders who represent the qualities that you want your community to emulate. Having diverse perspectives in forming core values is important to creating a foundation where all members feel as though they belong down the road.

2. **Brainstorm a large list.** Start broad and brainstorm all of your core value ideas. Give everyone time to think independently before coming together to share collectively.

3. **Refine and decide.** Narrow down your brainstormed list to a few key values that get to the heart of what you want your community to be. Encourage stakeholders to give input, either informally through discussion or formally through

voting. There is no definitive number of values that a community must have. I recommend choosing between three and seven. They should each represent a distinct quality and coalesce to create a larger picture of what your community stands for.

Once you have chosen your core values for the community, share them publicly and remind members about them often. Make them available on your website or group description. Include them in your guidelines. Share them at the start of every meeting and include them when you on-board or train leaders. Core values aren't something you can set and forget. They have to be continually discussed in order to be effective.

Mission, vision, and values takeaway questions:

- How do you want members to feel when they are a part of your community?
- Which communities do you feel have core values that resonate most strongly with you? How do they live out those values?
- What is considered acceptable behavior in your group? What is unacceptable?
- How do you hold people accountable when they violate your values or push you farther from your vision?

I know that it can be tempting to want to rush right into inviting members into your group or launching your first campaign, but starting with a clear mission, vision, and values is critical. It sets the tone. A community built on a strong foundation is built to last. That is why we start with mission, vision, and values.

2. Choose and nurture strong leaders.

A community is only as great as its leaders. The leaders of your community will directly shape the culture and the way members feel as they join and engage in the organization.

Choose your leaders with care.

Start by building a persona of who your ideal leader would be. Think about their ideal qualities and skill sets. Create a list of things that you want this person to be and the values they should uphold.

For example, I intentionally look for community leaders who are mission-driven, empathetic, diplomatic, resourceful, and deeply connected to our mission, vision, and values.

Once you've outlined who your ideal leader would be, think about the motivations for why someone might want to lead within your community and identify which factors are in alignment with your vision for leadership.

For example, some people might want to lead for the title or position of power. Others may be more motivated by the chance to make an impact or the feeling they get from helping a member reach their goals. Understanding potential motivators will help you to discern who is stepping up for the right reasons and what the value is that leaders will take away from the experience.

It is also important to construct a vetting process. Don't shy away from asking potential leaders tough questions. A strong leader can make or

break the experience that members have with a community, so it is impera-
tive that you choose the right people from the start.

Here are a few great questions to ask potential leaders during the vetting process.

- Why do you want to lead? What is your motivation for leading?
- Give an example of a time you dealt with interpersonal conflict.
  How did you navigate it? What was the outcome?
- How do you motivate others to take action?
- What is an area where you feel as though we can improve as a
  community?
- What impact would you like to make as a leader in our commu-
  nity?

For Rising Tide, our process of choosing leaders includes an online
application, a formal interview, and a rigorous onboarding process. Every
leader is educated on their roles and responsibilities before taking on the
title. This has evolved over the last six years as we have learned more about
what we need from our leaders and who is the best person for the job.

Allow your leadership selection processes to evolve over time, and
when you find a leader that is the ideal fit, think about why that is and
incorporate it into your persona. Improve your selections as you gather
more experience and insight.

Nurture from within.
When looking to choose leaders for your group, consider looking first
at your most committed members who demonstrate an interest in being

more involved. The best leaders often begin as passionate members who are nurtured into roles of leadership.

Create opportunities for deeper involvement (initiatives or campaigns where they can raise their hand), encourage members to take on more responsibility, and offer encouragement when you have an intuition that someone would be an excellent leader. Sometimes a small nudge or a word of affirmation can be the tipping point to encourage a member to rise up and lead.

Develop an intentional leadership model.

In order to empower people to be their best, feel fulfilled in their role, and provide as much value as possible to community members, develop an intentional leadership model. Think about the roles you need filled, the types of leaders who would best fill those roles, and clearly define responsibilities up front.

An intentional leadership model:

- Has specialized rather than general roles to empower leaders to leverage their unique personality types and superpowers. For example, you might need one leader to moderate your online group and another to plan events.
- Divides responsibilities to reduce burnout (especially for leaders in volunteer roles) and keeps workloads clearly defined and limited within the scope of each role.
- Contains opportunities for advancement as leaders grow and want to become more committed.

For example, at Rising Tide we have two primary leadership opportunities: leading local chapters and moderating our online Facebook community. Both local chapter leaders and online moderators must care deeply about our mission, vision, and values. They undergo leadership training to understand how our community operates and how we strive to create inclusive and equitable spaces where members can truly feel as though they belong.

The roles both moderators and chapter leaders play are specialized to their interests and superpowers.

Our moderators oversee conversations, manage pending posts, and make challenging decisions regarding content and violations to our guidelines. To be a moderator, you have to be good at conflict resolution, making hard decisions, and connecting with people online. The role is best for someone who spends a good amount of time online and is a natural at navigating Facebook group discussion throughout the day.

Our chapter leaders organize in-person events and are deeply involved in their local communities. To be a chapter leader, you have to be good at coordinating events, creating valuable programming, building face-to-face relationships, delegating responsibilities, and managing a team. This role is best for someone who is comfortable hosting in person and is great at motivating others to take on additional responsibilities.

Additionally, many of our local chapters have chair/committee positions that report to each local leader. This creates a stepping-stone into leadership and creates more opportunities to get involved as members become more invested in Rising Tide.

Creating an intentional leadership model means having specialized leadership roles, dividing responsibilities between those roles, and creating opportunities to advance in your community involvement over time.

Encourage integrity, not perfection.

We don't need our leaders to be perfect, but we do need them to have integrity. The best leaders hold themselves accountable and humbly admit when they could have done better. They learn from their mistakes, are open to critical feedback, and improve going forward.

Perfection is not the requirement—integrity to upholding core values, however, is.

3. Create shared experiences.

Here is where the mission, vision, and values collide with leaders who are able to make your community experiences meaningful for your members.

Shared experiences can be large or small, seemingly significant or insignificant in the grand scheme of the community experience. They can take place in person or online. They can originate organically or be planned proactively.

However, all shared experiences bring the community together and encourage members to connect with one another so that they can foster meaningful relationships or personal progress.

Shared experiences often take the form of rituals, events, traditions, and symbols—or REST.

Rituals

Events

Symbols

Traditions

Let's look at each individually.

Rituals

Rituals in the context of community are a set of practices that all members of a group engage in. This might look like shaking someone's hand as a greeting or singing "Happy Birthday" around a celebratory cake when someone gets a year older. In religious communities this often looks like prayers, hymns, and chants. In athletics it often looks like putting your hands in a circle for a collective "go team" cheer and concluding the game by shaking the other team's hands.

Rituals are the individual threads that knit us together in the tapestry of belonging.

Small and at first glance insignificant, rituals bring members closer together through a shared behavioral language or experience. Rituals are fundamental to community because they contribute to our sense of collective identity and cultivate meaning for all members of the group.

How to implement:

- Examine communities and groups that you are a part of and take note of the rituals that connect you to other members. What rituals do you notice? How do they make you feel? What do you suppose their purpose is?
- Ideate a few rituals that you can use to create a sense of collective identity and bring your community members closer together. What is the purpose of these rituals? How do you want them to make members feel?

Common rituals in community settings often include:

- A specific greeting when you walk through the door

- Reciting core values before the start of a meeting
- Kicking conversations off with an icebreaker
- A framework for introductions or taking the floor to speak

Rituals are as unique as the communities they arise from. These small actions lead to a feeling of belonging among members of the group.

Remember that rituals should serve to connect members closer together by building upon their sense of collective identity. They are contributors to the culture of your group and can transform the way members feel about themselves in the context of your community.

Group events

Events are one of the easiest ways to bring people together physically or virtually within your community. Events can be cyclical or part of a tradition—like holidays, monthly meet-ups, annual fundraisers, or seasonal festivals. Events can also be spontaneous or serendipitous, popping up as opportunities arise or the mood strikes.

How to implement:

- **Clearly define the goal or goals for your event.** How does it relate to your mission? What do you want members to take away? The best events bring value for the individual members and for the collective group. Think about the value you want to offer and how you can achieve that through creating a meaningful event experience.
- **Outline the parameters and create a plan.** Is it recurring or one time? Where and when will it take place? How can you ensure it is accessible to all members? Who do you need to

help you to pull the event together? Start small with your event framework and create a plan.

- **Mobilize your community to share and get involved.** Equip your community members with the tools they need to share about the event. Build a committee of event organizers or volunteers. Recognize leaders and volunteers before, during, and after the event to honor and encourage more help in the future.

  Need to increase attendance at your event? Ask members to personally bring one friend with them. A direct invitation (phone call, text, or direct message) can dramatically increase the likelihood of attendance because it is personal and creates a feeling of accountability.

  Need to increase awareness through social sharing? Hold a raffle. Each online share by a community member counts as an entry. Mobilize your members to spread the word and be your marketing engine.

- **Get feedback.** After an event, survey participants to collect feedback on what members liked and what you could improve upon. It is important to listen to feedback in order to continue fostering a sense of safety and belonging within your group.

Personally, my favorite group activities and events are those that create a little bit of intentional adversity and rivalry. You know, outings that present a slight challenge or difficulty that we can overcome together or in small teams. Bonds are often built by doing something difficult together. Healthy rivalry, as we know, also fosters a sense of belonging.

Here are a few examples of events centered around small doses of intentional adversity:

- Game nights, puzzles, and escape rooms
- Citywide or digital scavenger hunts
- Recreational sports or a group physical activity
- Learning a new skill or taking a class together
- Fundraising for charity or volunteering together for a cause you care about

Intentional shared experiences can jump-start bonding and create memories that you'll recount long after they are over. It can be as easy as choosing a group of friends, dividing into teams, and conquering a challenge.

When planning group events, ensure that everyone can participate by keeping accessibility in mind. At Rising Tide, this means offering online events in addition to in-person ones for people who cannot attend physical gatherings. It also means prioritizing accessibility (live transcription for webinars, captioning for pre-recorded videos, choosing buildings with wheelchair access, renting chairs without armrests, etc.) to make sure that everyone can take part in the experience and feel intentionally included.

Symbols

Symbols are the badges of belonging. They are visual markers that represent or affiliate with something else. In the case of communities, symbols are recognizable indicators of the groups to which we belong.

A brand sticker on a laptop, a flag on a front porch, a family crest, a cross worn on a necklace, or the emblem of an apple on the back of a phone—are all symbols that connect people to a community, brand, or ideology larger than themselves.

In building your community, you can leverage symbols as a way of bringing people together and uniting them under a common icon, color, stylistic element, or brand. Symbols connect our personal identity to that of the collective identity. It gives us a tangible way to signal to others that we are a part of a particular group. It visually communicates our association.

How to implement:

- **Build upon what already exists.** Think about the existing symbols that are already recognizable as part of your community. What do those elements signify? How do members engage with them? How can you build upon them?
- **Create new symbols.** Choose a visual element, icon, or even a hashtag that members can use to showcase to other members that they are a part of your group. Model how you want members to use your symbol and equip them with the tools (visuals, stickers, buttons, etc.) that they need to showcase their membership.
- **Make them a part of the community brand.** Incorporate symbols into the member or leader onboarding experience. Include them in outgoing communication (letterhead, emails, group banners). Ensure that your symbols are a part of your members' touchpoints with your community.

For example, members of the Rising Tide Society use our hashtags on their social media content as a symbol to other members that they share core values (#communityovercompetition), are a part of the same community (#risingtidesociety), and take part in the same gatherings

(#tuesdaystogether). That specific string of words signifies who is a member and cultivates a feeling of camaraderie between them.

In creating symbols for your community, start small. Choose one icon or visual element that you want members to use to showcase their affiliation with your community.

Remember to communicate the why behind the symbol as it should connect to your mission, vision, or values in some way. The most powerful symbols are those that are both recognizable and meaningful.

Takeaway questions:

- What symbols do you identify with most? Why do you think they are important to you?
- Are there symbols that you think connect you to a deeper sense of belonging? (What would stop your stroll or your scroll as your brain recognizes that symbol as a part of your identity?)
- How can you include symbols as a part of your community culture? What symbols signify the sense of belonging you are hoping to cultivate?

Traditions

Traditions are a long-established pattern of beliefs or practices. They create an anticipated set of events or customs that members of a community look forward to. By repeating, they also create a renewed sense of belonging over time.

As we cultivate community, we can actively and intentionally craft traditions that enable shared experiences to continue in a cyclical way into the future.

Every month at Rising Tide, we release a brand-new business guide on a topic that is important to our community members. *Marketing, sales, workflows, communications, client experience, accounting…you name it, we've covered it.*

However, once a year we dedicate ourselves to a topic unrelated to business—philanthropy and altruism. Instead of bonding face-to-face over a cup of coffee, we head out into the community and bond shoulder-to-shoulder.

We hold canned-food drives and build homes. We write cards for soldiers abroad and photograph rescue pups to help them find forever homes. Rising Tide members gather in cities all around the world to give back, and our entire community is made stronger for it.

Traditions can begin at any point in time and should evolve as a community grows. Just because you have had a family tradition since you were a child doesn't mean that you must carry it into adulthood. Likewise, just because your community has never tried a new tradition before doesn't mean you can't start something new.

It is also important to question whether existing traditions continue to align with your greater purpose as a community.

In *The Art of Gathering*, Priya Parker explains: "When we don't examine the deeper assumptions behind why we gather, we end up skipping too quickly to replicating old, staid formats of gathering. And we forgo the possibility of creating something memorable, even transformative."[1]

Several years ago, I was spending time with our Rising Tide leaders in Los Angeles after one of our first mega meet-ups. As we were walking to get lunch together after concluding our gathering, one of the leaders asked, "Why are we so quick to celebrate women when they get engaged, married, or pregnant but we have no rituals around celebrating when a woman starts a business? Shouldn't we be hosting 'business showers' too?"

Shoot. She was absolutely right. Sometimes we are quick to repeat formal traditions without questioning whether they are still relevant or connect to the individual or community need.

As a wedding photographer, I have witnessed many couples who have unraveled past traditions and created unique ones, forgoing outdated expectations in favor of more meaningful ways to celebrate their union uniquely.

It is empowering to acknowledge that we have control over the traditions that we are a part of in our lives and communities. We do not need to repeat traditions that no longer serve us. We can create new ones that are in deeper alignment with our purpose. The choice is ours.

How to implement:

- **Analyze existing traditions.** Look at existing traditions that you have in your family, workplace, or community. Are they still positively serving their purpose? How can they be changed or altered to bring about a more meaningful experience for all involved?
- **Brainstorm new ones.** Are there new opportunities to create impactful traditions in your group? Are there events that need celebrating or milestones that deserve to be honored? How can you make these new traditions meaningful and impactful?

Often in our communities we set out to solve pain points that people are feeling or provide value to help people achieve something in their lives.

Think about centering traditions around intentional moments, milestones, or collective days of celebration or reflection.

Traditions can create intentional intersection points that bring us back together and give us something to look forward to as we live in community with one another.

Takeaway questions:

- What traditions hold the most meaning for us in our homes, workplaces, and communities? Why do they have significance?
- Are there traditions that would be meaningful to start this year and continue into the future?
- Are there traditions that are no longer serving our gatherings that should be left behind in the pursuit of intentionally cultivating connection?

BUILDING COMMUNITY, TOGETHER

When a company lives by its mission, vision, and values, it can create so much more than a profitable business—it can truly form a family.

In the fall of 2015, we received an email out of the blue from a company called HoneyBook, a client management software. Their cofounders invited the Rising Tide team out to San Francisco to host our first gathering in the city.

We boarded a plane, flew out to California, and gathered around a table for lunch. Sitting together in a back room of the office, overlooking a shaded side street in the warehouse district of San Francisco, HoneyBook's CEO Oz Alon sat directly across from me over a plate of sushi.

He began to talk about his vision for the creative economy. I was captivated. Within minutes, we were all finishing each other's sentences.

We talked about how creative entrepreneurship was the future of work. How we believed in a matter of decades, technology would shift our economic infrastructure and start a modern industrial revolution…Oh! And it would be the creative ones: small-business owners, innovators, artists, and freelancers who led humanity into the future of work.

In order to support them, we all agreed that they needed two things:

1. The ability to focus on and invest in their superpowers (their craft, the thing that they were created to do and loved doing).
2. A community to support them through the challenges that lie ahead.

HoneyBook had set out to solve the first need, and Rising Tide had set out to solve the second. They were building technology. We were cultivating community.

They were fighting to free creatives and entrepreneurs from the manual processes involved in business management. We were fighting for belonging in a broken system—disrupting the way small businesses saw one another as competitors through cultivating impactful local communities.

We had slightly different missions; however, we shared the same vision. We both desired a reality where all people could build a life on passion and purpose. We both hoped for a world where creativity and entrepreneurship collided to lead us into the future.

What solidified our partnership, however, was what Oz shared next. Framed on the walls of that San Francisco office were HoneyBook's core values:

People come first.
We go the extra mile.
We love what we do.
We are fearless.
We are family.

I could see that we shared a lot more than just our vision of the future. We also shared values. There is something remarkable about aligning on values—it clarifies the opportunities that exist to build something better, together.

Rising Tide and HoneyBook joined forces that week and have been together ever since. A partnership built on a hopeful vision of the future and a foundation of shared core values. The incredible years that followed have turned my HoneyBook coworkers into my extended family.

In half a decade, we've shared countless experiences as a team. We start every week by gathering together and end it precisely the same.

We have hosted Whiskey Wednesdays and hustled side by side during hackathons. We've drafted petitions, created hundreds of pages of content, raised thousands of dollars for charity, and hosted events for tens of thousands of people.

And in hard times, we've always operated much like a family.

During my extended recovery from brain surgery, my HoneyBook coworkers stood in steadfast support of me through each hurdle and hardship. They brought meals to my apartment. They took work off my plate. They checked in on me every single day until I was well enough to return to work.

When the coronavirus pandemic struck our community down, we fought tooth and nail to save it. We rallied behind the small businesses that we believe in so strongly. Our sales team converted into a crisis-response team—ceasing business as usual to call our members one by one and ask how we could support them. Our marketers switched gears and began creating legal and financial resources to protect our members. Our Rising Tide leaders hosted town-hall-style gatherings to support members on the ground.

When small businesses saw their livelihoods threatened overnight, I watched my company live by our values. Putting people before profit, we stopped selling and started serving. We united as a family and rose to the occasion, even when it caused harm to the bottom line.

The months following the onset of the pandemic were some of our most successful as a business. Our community rallied around us, and our members advocated for us—feeling a deep sense of connection to how we supported them in their time of need.

If core values are the backbone of belonging, then living by them in hard seasons becomes the heartbeat of your business. Companies and communities built up from core values will emerge from the darkness, time and time again—united by so much more, dedicated to something greater.

As you set out to create something of your own, please remember: Start with vision, mission, and values. Choose leaders with intention. Cultivate experiences that bring your group closer together. Building stronger communities, better companies, more deeply connected families can have a profound impact on our world as a whole.

CHAPTER THIRTEEN

REJECTION AND REDEMPTION

A few years ago, I was speaking at an event in Washington, DC. It was my first time giving a talk of this magnitude alongside women I had looked up to for years. Frankly, I was terrified.

On the drive into the city, I recited my lines, running through my talk over and over again in my mind. I breathed in deeply, trying to replace the anxiety in my chest with sweet, sweet oxygen.

Get it together, Nat.

Walking into the auditorium, I noticed a few of the other speakers standing by the stage. I was intimidated. Do I just walk up and join them? Or do I hide backstage and continue to practice my presentation?

My hands were vibrating—clammy, jittery, like a downed power line after a thunderstorm.

My introverted tendencies got the best of me, and as I started to retreat, one of the women waved. *Shoot. She saw me.*

I wiped the sweat from my hands inside the pockets of my blazer and walked toward her by the side of the stage. We hugged and made small talk about the weather and the great turnout. A few others spotted us and joined the conversation. Our duo quickly became a huddle.

I recognized one of the women who walked up from years earlier. She was a photographer, like me, and we worked in a similar market. That's when I noticed her tattoos. We had connected only online in the past, and therefore, I never knew she had tattoos. I had just gotten my first one a few months earlier, after years of working up the courage to do it.

In an effort to connect, I awkwardly asked her about the significance of her tattoos. Everyone turned to listen. Her response piqued my interest. She made it all sound so easy as she recounted each bit of ink and the story behind it.

I remember thinking how she was a hell of a lot braver than I was. Getting a tiny tattoo on my ankle had felt like the decision of a lifetime. I agonized over it for ages, so afraid of what other people might think, whether they would judge me. Why couldn't I be more like her?

This girl was an absolute badass. I admired her guts.

Three years and what felt like a lifetime later, I was working late in our San Francisco office when I received a private message. It was the girl with the gorgeous tattoos, the photographer I'd met at a conference years prior.

We hadn't spoken once since that day in the auditorium, and I was excited to see why she was reaching out. I went back into my DMs and opened her message. It was a long message—too long. I scrolled and scrolled to get to the top. Something was wrong.

It took her three years to write me this message, and from the very first line, I felt my stomach drop to my feet, then melt right through the floor, and continue plunging into the depths of the earth. *No, no, no...*

In her own words, she recounted the interaction that day in the auditorium in a way that vastly contrasted with my memory. My compliment, through her eyes, was veiled criticism. She thought I was asking her about her tattoos because I didn't like tattoos and I was judging her for her choices. "You shattered my 'amazing' view of you. In a single moment I felt unworthy and critically judged," she wrote.

Ouch. Every part of me wanted to reach through the phone and tell her that she misunderstood. Tears started welling in the corners of my eyes, and a familiar ache of shame washed over me.

As someone who had spent much of her life feeling like the misfit, battling the figurative and, at times, literal, mean girls, the thought that I could make anyone else feel that way was downright heartbreaking. I had walked into the auditorium that day feeling like red-haired Cady Heron on her first day of school in *Mean Girls*, anxious and out of place, but to another woman, I was Regina-freaking-George.

I felt the shame spiral coming on....

How could she have thought I was judging her? Does she know that I also had a tattoo? She probably doesn't. I failed to mention it in the anxiety-riddled awkwardness of our conversation. Did she sense my nerves as something else? Did my nervous face make it look like I was judging her? How could she think that I was intentionally being mean?

She spent three years holding on to the pain of that interaction before feeling ready to tell me how deeply her perception of our interaction had hurt her. The words of her direct message wrecked me. I could only imagine how it had felt for her to carry that all those years.

I immediately responded and apologized. I asked for her forgiveness— not because my intent was ever to hurt her, but simply because despite having good intentions, I inadvertently had.

By now you've probably learned enough about me to know that I would never intentionally do anything to make someone feel that way. For as many flaws as I have, working to help others feel a sense of belonging is what I have dedicated my life to. Striving to cultivate community and relationships as an imperfect leader means that oftentimes I fail in the pursuit of creating connection.

However, regardless of the fact that my intentions were genuine, my execution left her feeling completely the opposite. My words had hurt her. That was all that mattered.

REJECTION

I struggled with whether or not to share that story. Frankly, I struggled with whether or not to write a chapter about rejection in a book about belonging.

It felt uncomfortable. It still feels uncomfortable. No one wants to recount a time when they made someone else feel judged or unwelcome. No one wants to remember a time in their past when they felt that way too.

However, at one point or another in our lives we will either: (a) be rejected or (b) leave someone else feeling rejected.

As humans, we are imperfect beings. Even with pure intentions, we are capable of causing harm. Even when we strive to create spaces of belonging, we run the risk of doing the opposite.

Sometimes we cannot anticipate the way others will interpret even our best-intentioned efforts to connect. Likewise, sometimes we will be on the receiving end of negative interactions, and it can be difficult to move forward when you've been hurt in the context of community.

Let me be clear: I am the first person to admit that I have made enough mistakes in this arena to write an entirely separate book about it. Many community leaders would tell you the same thing. When you step up to serve, you're bound to falter. However, with each misstep, we have an obligation to reflect, to learn, and to do better next time.

When we set out to create communities or engage in relationships, we must commit to being vulnerable. When we open our heart to the possibility of relationships, there is a chance that through that vulnerability, we will get hurt or that we will hurt someone else. I believe that the way we respond in these challenging situations is ultimately what defines our character.

Whenever I speak to groups of people about this subject, there is always someone who asks me about how to navigate negative past experiences in relationships. Feelings of rejection, competition, exclusion, and judgment are often in the top list of reasons someone is hesitant to commit to joining a community.

The same often applies to companies and organizations that leave employees feeling unsupported, unheard, and unappreciated. Negative feelings can fester and distrust can continue to follow us long after the initial damage is done.

When I talk about belonging and the importance of it, I am encouraging you to find or create healthy communities that work toward inclusion, respect, and empowering all members involved.

There are communities in this world that do not strive for those values. There are groups that embrace cultures of exclusion and divisiveness. There are organizations under unhealthy leadership that unite members through fear and anger rather than love and belonging. Avoid those spaces at all costs. A culture of exclusion anywhere is a threat to belonging everywhere.

However, as we all know, even in healthy communities where values are in alignment and all members are united by a shared purpose, negative experiences can arise. This is the nature of community. I've never seen a community where there hasn't been at least one instance of conflict or discord.

Especially when the internet is involved—every controversial subject is a tinderbox simply waiting for a spark. Keyboards are used to wage war, and real human beings struggle to cope when they are caught in the crossfire.

So how do we navigate hard experiences with others in community settings to prevent them from pushing us further into social isolation? How do we address rejection? How do we nurture more inclusive and welcoming spaces? Let's talk about it.

Communication is the key.

In setting out to foster welcoming communities, we must also proactively create a culture of open feedback and communication. This means intentionally fostering a spirit of openness about areas where we may be falling short or not living up to our aspired values.

In practice, this may look like giving and receiving feedback in real time and equipping leaders with the tools they need to facilitate these conversations well. Organizationally, this should include anonymous surveys that specifically address whether members feel as though they belong as well as facilitated feedback sessions with those who feel that there is room for improvement.

Welcoming, honoring, and intentionally responding to critical feedback sets the stage for dialogue that can truly change the direction of a company or community.

Likewise, in our personal relationships, this means that you must tell people when their words or actions hurt you.

Many of us have been socially conditioned to avoid directly addressing conflict. For example, I get a queasy feeling in my stomach when I think about telling someone else that they have hurt my feelings. However, we need to challenge ourselves to speak up and be communicative in difficult situations. (We'll discuss how to do this in just a bit.)

Choose the setting for communication wisely. Face-to-face is always preferred and prevents misinterpretations that often arise from reading written words without tone or eye contact. Rather than sending an email, consider hopping on the phone or getting together for coffee.

In an effort to seek resolution, avoid making assumptions about someone else's intentions and approach the conversation from a place of empathy. Give people a chance to share their heart and, whenever possible, extend grace.

Listen and use empathy as a vehicle to move the conversation forward. Countless times in community, choosing to communicate has repaired broken relationships before the situation dissolves irreversibly. Being honest also creates new opportunities for growth.

Behaviors that create a false depiction of resolution and are not ideal include:

- Avoidance of the situation entirely
- Internalizing hurt to spare others' feelings
- Modifying oneself in order to avoid future rejection
- Venting or gossiping about your experience with others

*When you've been hurt...*communicate early and often. Be direct. Be honest. Hold your ground and seek ways to repair the relationship when it is safe and possible to do so.

The process of healing begins when we are willing and encouraged to communicate how we feel and create an opportunity for others to commit to building something better together.

An open and honest practice of feedback, both in our communities and in our own relationships, can prevent instances of rejection from evolving into an overall culture of exclusion. Communication, especially in the context of difficult conversations, can transform the way we feel and engage with one another.

When you see or experience rejection, speak up.

We must call out exclusion when we see it. We cannot turn a blind eye to behaviors or systems that leave others feeling left out or unwelcome.

Likewise, we must also have the courage to express how we are feeling when we perceive rejection from others. We must be honest in moments when the actions of another person leave us feeling unwelcome, judged, or excluded.

A simple framework that works: "When you said/did <u>this</u>, it made me feel like…"

Then you pause and give them space to respond.

In doing so, we give that person an opportunity to take accountability, seek forgiveness, and grow from the experience. We may not always receive the answers or response that we are looking for, but we owe it to ourselves to communicate what we need and know what we deserve in our relationships with others.

How many times have others made you feel inferior or unwelcome? Did you tell them how those interactions made you feel? Did you speak up?

We can never assume that people know how they made us feel. More often than not, they are not aware of how they came across or how it impacted or harmed us.

While I was struggling with infertility, I had several interactions with women who were deeply wounding. Certain offhand comments made me feel excluded from a community that I yearned to be a part of.

You've been married for a long time…don't you want kids? If only you knew.

Hurry up and have a baby. You're not getting any younger. Ouch, thanks for reminding me.

At first I didn't know how to handle comments like those, so I would just stay quiet. My face would flush, and I would nod before sneaking away to release my feelings in private. However, since I never addressed the harm caused, the comments just kept coming (sometimes from the same people).

Eventually I realized that if I wanted a different outcome, I had to adjust my reaction. It wasn't enough to assume that others were aware of how their comments made me feel. I had to muster up the courage to address their words head-on.

"Actually, I'm battling infertility," I would say, and immediately their faces would change.

More often than not, they would backtrack and apologize. Some would even open up about their own struggles or the losses that they had endured along the way. By being honest and direct about my reality, I clarified to others how their words made me feel and created an opportunity to honor my own feelings and experiences.

Healing in moments of rejection often begins when we are able to directly address the interaction that left us feeling that way. It is important to state how something impacted you directly while being cautious to avoid assuming intent.

Speak from the heart and be direct. Honesty and vulnerability are the bridge between loneliness and belonging. When we are courageous enough to communicate what we expect from one another, we create opportunities for healing and redemption.

And remember, we cannot control the words and actions of others— only how we react to them. Speaking up when we feel rejected presents an opportunity for others to change their behavior, but it certainly does not guarantee it.

Addressing rejection head-on may not change how you have felt in the past, but it enables you to move forward and, in some cases, build a better relationship in the future.

Likewise, speaking up when you see exclusion or rejection may not heal the past harm done, but it is the only way to transform communities into more welcoming, inclusive spaces for the future.

Create your zero-tolerance policy.

A zero-tolerance policy serves to proactively discourage harmful behavior as well as to dictate the repercussions for harmful actions when they do occur. Every company, community, and organization should have one in place.

Likewise, in our personal relationships, we must also identify what we will not tolerate. You and only you know what behavior is acceptable in your interactions with others.

When a group enables competition to run rampant and allows members to push others down in order to succeed, it sets a precedent going forward, and the behavior will likely worsen. On the flip side, when someone speaks up swiftly and makes it clear that those behaviors are not acceptable, it sets a different foundation, from which the group grows.

Creating your zero-tolerance policy means you are holding yourself accountable for having hard conversations in the pursuit of honoring yourself and others. It's a powerful tool for preventing negative behaviors from turning into systemic problems within a community.

Remember that standing up for yourself and others is a muscle. The more often you exercise it, the easier it becomes to do in the future.

The first time you do it, it may be with trembling hands and a shaking voice. By the tenth time, you grow a sense of confidence in your ability to speak up. The goal should be to practice having these conversations and normalizing them as a part of your discourse.

Handling difficult discourse is important. The more often you do it, the more comfortable you become with having hard conversations.

Forgiveness is a gift to ourselves.

Sometimes when we are hurting, we find it hard to forgive. We carry pain with us from past relationships and interactions into our future experiences. Think of it like a subconscious weight that rests upon our shoulders. No matter where we go, it is always there making it just a little harder for us to carry on.

We bring our pain from rejection with us into future relationships. We carry it into new communities. It remains on our shoulders until we consciously begin the process of setting it down. And mark my words—forgiveness is a process.

You cannot snap your fingers and instantly forgive someone who has hurt or rejected you. It is a hard and often painful journey that unfolds over time. However, forgiveness is a critical part of our own self-care. It isn't so much about the person receiving forgiveness as it is about the person offering it and the impact that has on their well-being.

There are many misconceptions about forgiveness. Whenever I talk about it in the context of rejection and relationships, people are hesitant to fully embrace the necessity of this process. So let's get a few things straight.

Forgiveness is not:

- Condoning or exonerating the actions of another person
- Erasing their wrongdoing from your memory or pretending it didn't happen
- A renewal of trust or the complete restoration of a relationship

Forgiveness is about healing. Relinquishing your mind from the harmful clutches of animosity and pain. Choosing to consciously forgive also impacts your physical well-being and has been shown to reduce levels of stress, reduce cardiovascular problems, and improve immune system performance.[1]

Forgiveness also provides freedom. In order for us to move forward into spaces where we truly feel seen, heard, and valued, we must let go of the resentment and bitterness of past rejection. We can acknowledge the hurt that someone has caused us without letting that pain rob us of future joy. That is a powerful notion.

Forgiving doesn't mean forgetting. Forgiving means moving forward, and it is a profound gift that we give to ourselves.

WHEN YOU HURT SOMEONE, ACCEPT RESPONSIBILITY AND APOLOGIZE

Let's look at this from the other side. Sometimes we are going to hurt others unintentionally. This is a messy part of engaging in relationships and community with others. It doesn't matter how sincere you are heading into an interaction—pain can arise from the most innocent of conversations.

Now, I don't say this to scare you or to make you overanalyze all of your previous interactions with others. *Kick that shame spiral to the curb right now!* I raise this point because how we respond in moments when we have hurt someone matters.

We have a choice. We can choose to write it off, dismiss the experiences and feelings of another person as our ego often baits us to do…or we can accept responsibility and choose to genuinely apologize. We can get angry and defensive. We can choose to list out all the reasons they are wrong and we are right…or we can empathize with their experience, acknowledge how we hurt them, and seek forgiveness.

I think you know which direction I'm leaning toward here: accept responsibility and apologize. So how do we do that, exactly?

First, I believe it is important to acknowledge bravery when we see it in others. It isn't easy for many of us to be open about our feelings. Telling someone that they have hurt you isn't on anyone's top-ten list of favorite conversations.

When we have the opportunity to affirm vulnerability and applaud courage, we must do it. Especially in moments when someone else might be anticipating the opposite. How we respond influences whether someone's hurt leads to additional trauma or creates an opportunity for mutual resolution. It may sound something like:

"Thank you for having the courage to share that with me. I am so grateful that you did."

"I had no idea that you were feeling that way.... Thank you so much for being so vulnerable and coming to me directly."

Then, it is important to acknowledge the harm done—address it directly and do your best not to respond dismissively or defensively. Apologize genuinely and conclude by asking how to rectify the situation if necessary.

"I am so sorry that I made you feel that way. It was never my intention. What can I do to make this right?"

Three short sentences that open a door to something better. Accepting responsibility for unintentional harm does not make you a bad person. It makes you a kind person. It demonstrates love and self-awareness. It showcases integrity.

When we hurt someone, our response sets the tone for the remainder of that relationship. Apologizing is not accepting defeat, but rather the opposite. Apologizing creates an opportunity for the ultimate shared victories that we aspire to achieve: restoration and redemption.

None of us wants to live with the pain of rejection holding us back from the beautiful experiences that community has to offer. In order to move forward, we must be willing to create open dialogues with one another and be receptive to feedback. We need to leave our egos at the door and keep our hearts centered on empathy and forgiveness.

When you make mistakes, own them, apologize, and learn from the experience. When you are hurt, speak up and be clear about how the interaction made you feel.

Additionally, companies and communities that desire to facilitate a strong culture of belonging should train all leaders and members on how to navigate these conversations, accept responsibility for harm caused, and proactively work to repair conflict.

With a foundation of honesty and clear communication, we can work together to navigate difficult conversations and challenging circumstances as they arise. We can see the glimmers of hope on the horizon, where transgressions are forgiven and relationships are redeemed.

CHAPTER FOURTEEN

THE TRUE ROI OF COMMUNITY

When you move into the professional community-building world, you are quickly made aware of just how challenging it is to prove the value of community. In boardrooms and in budget meetings, all community leaders are asked a fair and yet frustrating question: What is the ROI of community?

In a nervous rush, we hustle back to our data dashboards, searching for evidence of what we already know to be true. We lean into metrics that measure scale, engagement, adoption, sentiment, and churn—all the while recognizing that no single number truly quantifies the impact of having a strong community. We field questions from executives determining where budget allocations will go and often leave feeling defeated because when something's value is challenging to quantify, broad buy-in is difficult to achieve.

How many members does the community have? How engaged are they?

Are they contributing to growth? What is the return on the investment of start-ing, cultivating, and nurturing a community? Is it truly worth the cost for the company?

The intersection of relationships and transactions is becoming an increasingly blurred line in modern commerce. Consumers vote with their dollars. When customers feel deeply connected to a brand, more than half will increase their spending with that company and three-fourths will buy from them over a competitor.[1]

Companies either thrive or fail based on the relationships they cultivate with their customers. We live in a time when every person has a platform, every voice is heard, and you either understand the power of community or you don't.

To many consumers, a brand's values are equally as important as the quality of their product. Connection and social capital are the new currency. The way companies show up for their community and connect customers to one another matters more than ever before.

It is no longer enough to have a good product. To truly stand out, you must deeply understand your people and have the power to mobilize them.

One successful company that can attribute much of its growth to the loyalty of its community is Airbnb.[2] The power of their platform to unite hosts and guests alike through both virtual and in-person connection has contributed to their rapid growth.

In order to fully understand the impact of community on Airbnb's trajectory, we have to rewind to a time before ride-sharing and home-swapping were commonplace. It is hard to imagine it now, but when Airbnb first launched, their service was a difficult sell.

Imagine trying to start a company whose success relies on convincing customers that they should skip booking a trusted hotel room and instead rent a space in a stranger's home in a foreign city where they have never been before.

I can still hear my mom in my ear as a kid saying "Don't talk to strangers!" and now you're trying to convince me to sleep in a stranger's bed in a city where I know no one?

Airbnb's growth was far more revolutionary than we give it credit for. The concept alone was countercultural, and the legal challenges of enabling short-term rentals in cities around the world meant going up against hospitality industry giants and sometimes even the law.

Airbnb's global head of community at the time, Douglas Atkin, was instrumental in turning the tide in the company's favor through changing public sentiment and mobilizing community activism.

He started by centering the entire brand around community—both through product and communications. The Airbnb platform itself housed forums where hosts could share knowledge and connect with one another. The hosts no longer felt alone. They were connected. They felt supported.

Information was shared around how to be a better host, how to take better photos of your listing, and how to encourage guests to leave reviews after their stay (among countless other critical bits of advice).

The ecosystem of hosts supporting hosts enabled the entire community to rise together. By sharing knowledge, they collectively were able to raise the quality of the service they were offering, and guests took notice. Airbnb gained favor among travelers as a personalized and authentic alternative in an increasingly commoditized world.

Additionally, Douglas Atkin's "Belong Anywhere" campaign challenged preconceived hesitancies to trust, to travel, and to feel at home in the houses of others.

The campaign asked all of us to remember the origins of humanity—

the villages where we all once knew our neighbors, the time before indus-
trialization. It connected our innate desire to belong and to feel connected
with a platform that offered to facilitate that experience once again. Airbnb
positioned itself as a brand of the people, by the people, for the people.
Atkin humanized the company by grounding it in community.

In a post about the Belong Anywhere campaign, Airbnb shared:

> For so long, people thought Airbnb was about renting houses.
> But really, we're about home. You see, a house is just a space,
> but a home is where you belong. And what makes this global
> community so special is that for the very first time, you can
> belong anywhere.[3]

As sentiments around peer-to-peer rentals changed and the platform
grew, it was met with legal challenges making it difficult for hosts to operate in certain cities. Using techniques founded in grassroots organizing,
Airbnb invited hosts and guests to become a part of the political advocacy
required for a peer-to-peer economy to flourish. By rallying members to
become leaders and step into the political arena, Airbnb overturned several
restrictions and went on to change the way we travel.[4]

Companies like Airbnb illustrate that community can transform the
trajectory of a business. When people unite around their passion for a
brand and a shared vision of the future, they are capable of doing remarkable things.

Community has the power to transform business outcomes.

Then, you may be wondering, with such a deep understanding of its
inherent value, why is it still difficult to measure the ROI of community? I

believe it comes down to this: the ROI of community cannot be summed up in a single metric.

That's not to say that there aren't valid indicators of success or numbers that clarify whether a community is having a profound impact or not, but to presume that we can adequately quantify the value of human connection and the power of people uniting is a dangerous assumption.

Think about the subconscious influence of social proof, the power of a single referral or personal recommendation, and the roaring advocacy of a passionate member base that can all influence the trajectory of a business. Community isn't just a marketing play or an acquisition strategy. Investing in this work impacts all points of the customer lifestyle—from top-of-funnel awareness to conversion to retention and churn.

Therefore, when we attempt to settle on a single metric to quantify the ROI of something that is so complex and inextricably woven into every aspect of the human experience, it should come as no surprise that we often fall short in trying to understand the magnitude of community's impact in our professional lives.

Additionally, should we choose to track the wrong metrics, we run the risk of romanticizing numbers that sound good to executives but fail to truly align with the genuine impact driven. For example, caring more about size and scale than engagement and retention.

Let's look at this through a lens that you have likely experienced firsthand.

When you turn on your phone and open your social networks, what are some of the first things you see at the top of your profile? Numbers.

Our world assigns numbers to people in an attempt to quantify their value. Followers, likes, and comments become the success metrics of modern relationships. These elements of our online personas become so inflated with value that we begin to obsess over vanity metrics rather than concentrating on what truly matters.

Every post becomes one more step in the race that we run for our worth and value. We create and curate our lives just to rank higher—rather than celebrating and cherishing the moments as they exist. With followers as a framework for earning influence, we focus our attention on counting and collecting people rather than understanding and valuing them as individuals. We constantly strive to find more friends rather than working to foster deeper connections with the ones we already have.

By prioritizing vanity metrics, we begin to overlook the qualities that truly matter. Attempting to quantify connection emphasizes the wrong things. We begin to prioritize incorrectly. We go off course.

As a result, we aim for:

Popularity over purpose
Quantity over quality
How things look over how things are

So herein lies the challenge. Community drives value—most would agree on that fact. Determining that ROI and understanding where impact is felt most strongly within the business is where we have to take a deeper look to ensure we aren't underestimating or missing the mark.

A MEASUREMENT MODEL

Quantifying the impact of community is hard, but it's certainly not impossible. I have spent more than five years professionally building and scaling communities both in person and online. Being data-driven is critical to monitoring the health of your community, understanding the success of your efforts, and communicating your impact cross-functionally to gain broader support.

While every professional community will set out to serve a different purpose, I generally recommend building your own measurement model that analyzes business impact across one or more of the following three sectors: growth, retention, and advocacy.

Additionally, whenever there is an opportunity to dive into the qualitative impact stories and member highlights that showcase the power of community in action, it is critical to do so. Not only does it provide color to the metrics you measure, but it often helps to connect other employees to the people that they serve, deepening their empathy and inspiring their work.

Growth

A thriving community is fuel to the fire when a company has product-market fit. From the power of a single testimonial, to the virality of social media, to the influence of user-generated content on buying behavior, a passionate community drives growth.

Thankfully, for professional community builders, growth is often the most enticing metric for executives when considering where to allocate budgets and build teams. (So, don't shy away from measuring growth from the outset…especially if you want more resources to invest back into your community!)

Additionally, for start-ups still building their products or companies working to refine their offerings, community input can serve as the vehicle for feedback that increases conversion in the long run.

When you know your customer and you deeply understand their

pains, you have a competitive advantage in the marketplace. From beta groups to customer surveys, engaged user communities can bubble up critical feedback that shifts the trajectory of the business and leads to long-term growth. It also provides insight on what your customers care about and how you can better serve them through product, content, or programming.

Metrics to consider:

- Percent of new users attributed to community channels
- Number of leads acquired through user-generated content/ community initiatives
- Number of product ideas implemented from the community
- Engagement markers across community groups and channels

A word of wisdom: build data infrastructure that tracks multi-touch attribution. Just because someone purchases a product through a sales promotion or ad doesn't mean they haven't been nurtured by the community prior to hitting the buy button. Being able to track leads as they engage with community initiatives is critical to understanding overall impact.

Additionally, it isn't uncommon for growth-related community impact to be misattributed to other channels, especially when initiatives intersect or platforms are shared. For instance, community groups hosted on Facebook are easily misattributed as inbounding from Facebook pages or hearing about the company from a marketing campaign rather than a community-led conversation. The battle for proper attribution will always be there within marketing and community teams. However, having visibility into various community touchpoints can make all the difference.

Retention

Customer retention is critical to the health of any business. Community can play a large role in improving activation and reducing churn by crowd-sourcing product education and democratizing customer support in a way that drives positive sentiment and reduces costs to the company.

I've seen this especially evident in customer success communities. Customer support does not need to be limited to chatbots, help centers, and one-on-one concierge care. Empowering passionate users to share about the product, showcase creative ways they are using features, and answer other members' questions creates more opportunities for swift resolution and user success. It can also reduce inbound support tickets and make members feel more supported and likely to stay.

Facebook communities are a common way for tech companies to cultivate relationships between customers and encourage them to share knowledge and best practices. Udemy, for example, has invested heavily in creating a Facebook group for its course creators. Community members advise one another, ask questions, and share what course ideas they are working on. After analyzing the impact of their Facebook community, Udemy found that instructors are four times more likely to create a course if they're part of the Facebook group.[5]

Likewise, Sephora stands out in the highly competitive cosmetics space with a thriving community of people interested in beauty. From sharing makeup hauls to clean beauty favorites to advice for how to handle acne-prone skin, their in-product community is packed with engaging conversations and user-generated content. Sephora's Beauty Insiders deeply humanizes the makeup giant and creates a deepened sense of loyalty among customers.[6]

How much loyalty? Sephora's highest-engaged community members spent an average of 36.5 hours on Beauty Talk weekly and spent more than ten times at Sephora than the average customer.[7]

They are superfans for the long haul, and this has a deep impact on customer retention.

Metrics to consider:

- Customer satisfaction or Net Promoter Score (NPS)
- Percentage of increased feature adoption with community-led education + content programming
- Percentage of community members engaging (contributing content/answering questions) in user groups
- Reduced number of support tickets; reduction in support costs due to community-led support

Advocacy

Passionate super-fans have the ability to generate an organic marketing engine that runs itself. We've all seen the impact of community-led virality and advocacy. Many of the products we've purchased have been recommended from friends or spotted in groups we're a part of online. Referrals and recommendations matter.

A great example of community advocacy through referrals can be found in an email newsletter company called the Skimm.

The company lovingly named their community advocates Skimm'-bassadors and has united members around a shared identity and love for the brand. Skimm'bassadors are equipped with a cheat sheet to maximize their effectiveness and have the opportunity to win swag for inviting others to join the newsletter. By exciting, nurturing, and mobilizing members with the tools they need to refer, the Skimm has directly turned the power of community into an advocacy engine.[8]

Although referral and affiliate programs are some of the most widely accepted ways of transferring community loyalty into business impact, it is certainly not the only way.

Advocacy can also be earned through extraordinary customer service that inspires a community to share about a brand in meaningful ways. One of my favorite examples of this is from a pet retailer called Chewy. Known for shipping pet products directly to your door, this company has built a cult following on how it serves its community.

When a mistake is made and an incorrect product ships, Chewy offers a refund and encourages its customers to donate the unwanted items to an animal shelter. When a longtime customer experiences the loss of their pet, Chewy employees are known to send flowers and heartfelt condolences. Neither of these actions is expected. However, they demonstrate a shared sense of core values between the brand and its customers.

Over the past decade, the company has become one of the most successful pet brands in the world. Founder Ryan Cohen launched the brand in 2011, then sold it to PetSmart six years later for $3.5 billion—noted as the largest e-commerce acquisition at that time. In the years since, their valuation has only continued to rise by billions and billions of dollars.

When talking about why the brand has had such tremendous success, Cohen notes: "When people shop at Chewy, they really understand we care about them, we care about their pets."[9]

The effort required to earn someone's trust will always be worth more than the practice of buying their attention. In business as it is in life, a personal recommendation carries a significant amount of weight, and when seeking to understand the impact of community, it is a vital thing to track.

Metrics to consider:

- Percentage of referrals (conversions or activations); percentage of referral links shared
- Conversion rate of referred customers versus organic inbounds
- Percentage of referring community members
- Percentage likelihood of a customer to refer based on being a community member

Additionally, I recommend monitoring brand sentiment and awareness indicators as part of understanding the power of community advocacy. Even if it is as simple as documenting anecdotes and qualitative input from community groups and social media platforms, it is critical to communicate the power of advocacy on brand and customer sentiment.

ROI EXPANDED

We've talked about building communities to fuel company growth, but what about looking within? When we set out to foster a deeper sense of belonging in our companies, neighborhoods, and organizations, what is the resulting impact?

You don't have to be a professional community builder to contemplate these questions. Arguably, as actively engaged human beings, we should constantly evaluate whether our actions are contributing positively to our lives and to the lives of others. That includes our time spent engaging and investing in relationships.

Although difficult to quantify, it remains intuitively understood that what we take away from the spaces where we belong and the connections that we cultivate is significant.

When we are deeply connected, we are:

- Heard, seen, and valued
- A part of something greater than ourselves
- Supported physically and emotionally in our lives
- Consciously aware of the needs of others
- Empowered to reach our potential

Radha Agrawal argues in her book, *Belong: Find Your People, Create Community, and Live a More Connected Life*, that the importance of belonging is so critical to our existence that it is in fact a fundamental human need in the same category as food, water, touch, love, and shelter. In reconstructing Maslow's original hierarchy of needs, Agrawal clarifies that "Without a community supporting you at each level, it's nearly impossible to move up the hierarchy."[10]

To rise and thrive, we need one another. As a result, we see connection woven into all aspects of those critical needs and our ability to move into higher levels of personal and professional development.

When you look at a successful individual and ask "How did they do it?" the world is quick to point to their individual accomplishments and personality traits: their degrees, the hours they spent honing their skills, their resilient mindsets, inherent intelligence, et cetera.

However, in my experience, the community infrastructure around the individual is just as important as the work they put into their own trajectory.

Who affirmed their self-esteem and built their confidence?

Who nurtured their resilience and modeled perseverance in their life?

Who sacrificed for them? Who still sacrifices for them?

Behind every successful human being is a person or people who introduced them to their power and potential. Connection and collaboration are the keys to developing into the people we were always meant to be.

The same truth applies to our companies and organizations. When we look at a successful brand, our world places far too much value on the actions of top-level executives in the C-suite without taking into account the impact that company is making on the ground floor.

Do employees feel deeply connected to the brand mission, its leaders, and one another?

Do the customers feel supported, valued, and well served?

Is the company connection centric in all aspects?

Google spent two years analyzing what made a successful team and found that the most important dynamic to fuel progress was psychological safety. In order for a team to be successful, members must feel safe to take risks and be vulnerable with one another. It didn't matter how many Rhodes Scholars and brilliant engineers they could cram into the same room if none of them felt safe to bring their entire selves to work. A sense of connection to people and values is critical.

Two other important team dynamics that Google found in its analysis included employees feeling a sense of meaning in their work and fundamentally believing that the work they do matters.[11] In many companies, this also ties to the power of community. Having the ability to connect with the customers you serve and see how your daily contributions positively impact their lives transforms the way you think about work.

Part of my role as head of community at HoneyBook is to serve as the bridge between our members and our employees. Sharing impact stories, highlighting "customer love," and showcasing the way our product is transforming businesses and livelihoods is important. When an engineer knows that a new feature has the ability to save a single mother two hours a week on a task she previously was doing manually in her business, it turns lines of code into a clear vision of a life transformed.

Community is not a buzzword to drive employer branding campaigns or recruit new hires. It must be a lived value for companies that desire to build high-performing teams of deeply fulfilled employees. Feeling profoundly connected to the work that we do and the people who are a part of our professional lives is important.

Investing in community and connection within an organization cannot be a quick strategy or a one-off effort. It cannot be an afterthought. It must be knit into the fabric of our company cultures just as it is knit into the fabric of our DNA.

A shout into the void.

What does a group of entrepreneurs, a Canadian *Bachelorette* contestant, and a wedding have in common? One of my favorite lighthearted stories about the power of community showcases just how unifying our willingness to help one another can be.

A few years ago, a random post in the Rising Tide Society Facebook group turned our entire community upside down. I'm talking zero to sixty, pedal to the floorboards, all business as usual ceased in a matter of minutes.

It is important to note that in groups of this size, it isn't entirely uncommon that a conversation will go viral....However, it was the first time we had experienced anything of this magnitude.

Rising Tide member and Texas photographer Stephanie Nelson was desperate to find a date to an upcoming wedding. Not sure where else to look, she took to social media and started searching for the perfect partner.

"Are there any handsome single guys that live in the Austin or San

Antonio area and are free this Saturday? My wedding date bailed," she posted.

Oh, and that wasn't all....This wasn't just an ordinary wedding. The stakes were particularly high for this event. *Why might that be?*

"It's my EX-BOYFRIEND'S wedding," she wrote. "I can't show up without a date and let his family see me all single and alone."

As if in unison, the entire community responded to the tune of: *Oh, heck no! We aren't going to let that happen. There is no way you are going to that wedding alone. Not on our watch!*

Stephanie's words became a passionate call to arms—within minutes an army of other business owners came rushing to her aid. They started calling friends and family members, reaching out to anyone and everyone to see who would be available on such short notice. The wedding was a few days away, and therefore searching for the perfect date became the community's primary goal.

We were going to find Stephanie someone incredible to take to this wedding. No matter what.

Ten comments...

Fifty comments...

One hundred comments...

One thousand comments...

It wasn't long before this particular post was being reshared in industry groups all across social media. My entire newsfeed became an amalgamation of separate conversations instructing people to go into the Rising Tide group and join our collective search to find Stephanie a date.

Within a few hours of the post going live, a fellow Rising Tide member added Kyle Skinner to the group.

Kyle, a former contestant on *The Bachelorette Canada*, was volunteered by his longtime friend, and he kindly agreed to be Stephanie's date to the wedding. The group went wild. We were so close to making this happen.

There was only one problem. And with the event approaching quickly, it was a big one.

Kyle lived thousands of miles away. He was in Canada and the event was in Texas.

However, the community wasn't going to let that stand in the way of this potential fairy-tale romance. Within minutes, members from all over the world started pitching in to pay for Kyle's plane ticket.

Five dollars from a photographer in Colorado.
Twenty dollars from a designer in Kansas.
Fifteen dollars from a freelancer in Florida.

When it was all said and done, nearly two thousand dollars flooded into a GoFundMe account to bring the pair together. The community erupted with excitement. *We did it!* We secured Stephanie's date!

A few days later, Kyle hopped on a plane, and the two walked into that wedding as we all cheered them on from afar. Photos were posted. Snapchats were shared. All eyes were on this infamous wedding.

Stephanie and Kyle shared every moment of their date night with us, and our entire group celebrated. Who would have thought that a group of small-business owners from all around the world would take such pride in helping a girl from Texas secure a date to an ex-boyfriend's wedding? [12]

It seems insignificant and perhaps a bit silly, but this moment became one of the hallmark memories that I think about when looking back on the past six years of leading Rising Tide.

Why? It demonstrates something important about the value of

community. One shout into the void—that's all it takes to rally a community into action. A seemingly standard problem solved by a group of strangers who didn't want one of their own to have to endure a difficult situation all by herself.

I've seen this same scenario played out over the years. Hardships big and small are solved by the collective efforts of the community. People helping people, ensuring that no one has to face this life alone. It doesn't always fit into the lighthearted framework of the story that I shared above. More often than not, we are reminded that community shines brightest in the darkest moments of our lives.

A business owner struggling to make ends meet—met by a flood of referrals and volunteers offering to help her improve her marketing strategies.

A chronic illness warrior searching for a friend who would empathize with the battle—met by a community of extraordinary humans that understood.

A military mother discovering that her family is being redeployed to the opposite side of the country and that she would have to rebuild her business from the ground up—met by a group of military entrepreneurs ready to support her every step of the way.

A pandemic sweeping across the country—met by countless people stepping up to support small businesses as the world went under siege.

A community leader diagnosed with a benign brain tumor, facing surgery—met by a community who carried her through the darkest season of her life.

All of these stories originate from a single community—our community, the Rising Tide Society. Each vignette represents a person's life made better by the collective. Each anecdote demonstrates a small glimmer of the total impact that community can bring.

There are millions of communities around the world. Millions of people helping one another to live life to the fullest. Groups uniting cancer survivors and single mothers, activists and advocates, dreamers and doers. In person and online—connected by big threads and little threads. The intersections of human connection are all around us.

When we seek to understand the value of community, we must look at each individual life improved by the existence of the whole. We must value each story and every connection. We must see the ways that connection has shaped us and impacted our lives. It will always be larger than a single measurement or metric....However, it is the place where we must begin.

> **The intersections of human connection are all around us.**

OUR MANIFESTO

I will never forget the first time I received a phone call telling me that our community had deeply impacted someone. I was working late in our Annapolis office when one of our local leaders called me out of the blue. The cars were rushing past on West Street, heading home for the day in rush-hour traffic. My husband was waiting at home, and as was common in those days, I was already late for dinner.

My phone sat buzzing beside my laptop. I answered. I will forever be grateful that I answered.

Earlier that day, a member had stayed late to talk with one of our local leaders long after the monthly Rising Tide meet-up was over. A vulnerable expression of loneliness was met with compassion as two strangers bonded. They talked about life and about how hard it was to carry the weight of the world on their shoulders. Walls came down and friendship was forged.

From the outside looking in, it sounded like a simple conversation. However, through the lens of that leader, it was a transformative experience.

"I felt the need to tell you…This community has saved my life."

I'll never forget hearing those words. It stopped me completely in my tracks. My eyes welled with tears. My hands trembled. I remember thinking:

She was the reason—the purpose behind all of it. Her life. That's it. She is the one that we were created to serve.

Nothing will ever strip away my fundamental belief that if everything I have done with Rising Tide was to improve that one person's life, then it was so much more than enough. I mean that literally, and I believe it with my entire heart.

The legacy of a community cannot be determined by its highlight reel. The value of a relationship cannot be measured in likes or followers. A number just can't quantify the impact of connection when human lives are on the line.

Over my lifetime, I've come to understand that the value of community is woven into the stories of every human being whose life was made better as a result. Every conversation, every intersection where two trajectories crossed and two lives would never be the same.

We belong to one another. Our lives are inextricably intertwined. How we treat the people around us has a profound effect on the collective success of our species.

When the world is watching and when it is not, in public and in private, in our hearts, our homes, our communities, choosing belonging builds a better tomorrow.

We see evidence of this all around us, and yet it barely scratches the surface of just how deeply we are impacted by our decisions to connect or withdraw. Every day is another opportunity to cultivate connection and build others up.

The impact of one brave act of connection multiplies exponentially. It starts as a single thought, a hand raised, a whisper, a spoken word.

It starts as a single voice shouting out into the darkness—*I am tired of feeling so alone*—and the unrelenting outcries of thousands of others who were also tired of longing for connection in the chaos.

One becomes two, and a movement is born, the voices of the collective illuminating the way forward: "We are tired of being alone too. We are tired of competing and comparing. We are ready to chart a course for our lives that brings us back to one another…that brings us back to where it all began."

We are created for connection because it is through connection that we come to exist in the first place. Community shapes us. Belonging betters us. When we are supported by others, we rise to heights as a collective that we once believed were impossible.

There is no doubt that our world threatens to tear us apart. When competitor is pitted against competitor, human against human, life often feels like a constant race to the top. Individual achievement is valued higher than collective prosperity. Mindsets of scarcity are weaponized against the hearts of humans who are yearning for connection.

We have no choice but to fight back. We must flip the script and turn the tide. We must vow to do better and to be kinder to ourselves and to one another. We must consciously eradicate narratives that push us farther into our separate corners.

We must reach out a hand and lift others up, elevating livelihoods and amplifying voices. We must surrender our need to be the best and concentrate on being our best. We must commit to learning, evolving, and making the road a little easier for the ones who come after us.

We cannot let loneliness overtake us. Like waves in a storm, the challenges will arise, and yet we must always press on. We cannot let go of the helm. We cannot give up the ship.

When confronted with seasons of struggle, we must look to one another and say, "You aren't alone. It may feel that way right now, but we're going to change it. I've got you. Come along, friend. We are going to get through this together."

We must let connection lead the way.

I want to end this book with a manifesto. It only felt appropriate to share one final call to arms, an outcry against our culture of self and endless competition. Consider this my personal declaration of war against the way things are and my deepest desires for the way things could be.

As you turn these final pages, I need you to raise your hand and commit to the possibility of building a better future, together.

You may be sitting with this book in hand wondering how your actions could possibly be enough to change the way things are. You may be questioning how large of an impact you will have. You may be worrying about whether your actions will truly make this world a better place.

I'm here to tell you that you could be the catalyst that changes everything. Your kindness, your voice, your actions going forward could make all the difference in the lives of others. Never doubt that in your efforts to connect, you could save someone else's life.

In order to cultivate belonging and champion a mindset of community over competition, you must step beyond the pages of this book to make actionable change. Are you with me? I invite you to join me in making this pledge.

I hereby pledge to:

- Challenge my own internal dialogues that leave me feeling less than, left out, and lonely; reframe my thoughts so that they lead me deeper into connection with others.
- Keep competition rightly ordered below community, putting people first in all things.
- Set aside comparison to truly cheer for others—not only when it is easy, but especially when it is hard.
- Tear down the walls around my heart and take off the masks that I wear in order to allow vulnerability to become a bridge to connection and belonging.
- Take a critical look at the spaces I occupy and the communities I am a part of to ensure that they are inclusive; use my voice to advocate for and celebrate diversity.
- Approach others with empathy, compassion, and kindness; look for ways to lift all boats and raise the tide for the collective.

I invite you to lean into the gifts that you have to offer this world and to share them abundantly with others. I encourage you to intentionally make a difference in someone else's life. It doesn't have to be a grand gesture or a major action—it can start small and build from your daily decisions in the communities that you are already a part of.

I encourage you to cultivate connection. Be the reason that someone else feels like they belong. Be their advocate in a world constantly trying to tell them that they aren't good enough.

Remind them that they matter, that their story matters and their voice matters and their life matters. Cheer for them. Affirm their strengths.

Amplify their voice. Celebrate their wins and walk alongside them through their struggles.

Don't be afraid to show them your scars—be vulnerable when you speak about your failures. Take off the mask you wear to hide your brokenness and your flaws. Surrender the need to be perfect—choose instead to be honest. Let people in. Serve as the safe harbor, the cheerleader, and the champion that so many in this world need.

Be the person who puts community over competition and champions a mindset of abundance. Honor the people who have helped you to reach the success you have today by making the journey easier for others.

Be an encourager of kindness and an empowerer of action. Rise up. Stand up. Show up. Be the best version of you and seek to inspire others to be the best version of themselves.

And above all else, remember that you were born to belong. You were created for community, and it is built directly into your DNA. Your voice, your perspective, your passion, your talents are needed in this world.

Show up exactly as you are, and through your courage, you will inspire others to do the same.

ACKNOWLEDGMENTS

The list of people whom I need to thank is a long one. I could fill pages upon pages without ever coming close to articulating my immense gratitude for the countless individuals who have made this book possible.

To my husband, Hugh. Thank you for taking my hand at fifteen and never letting go. You held it on our wedding day and the day we cofounded Rising Tide. You held it the day neurosurgeons told me that it was time to operate and every single day of recovery that followed. You held my hand when we started fertility treatment and when I was in labor with Huey, afraid of bringing our son into the world a month early; you held my hand through every contraction until those hands finally held our baby boy.

No matter what our future holds, I know that you will always reach out your hand and I will always take it. That's our thing. It will always be our thing. I love you and am so deeply grateful for you.

To our Rising Tide leaders, past and present. I asked if it would be possible to list all 800+ of you by name, but this will have to do. You will carry this legacy forward and have made Rising Tide more than I ever dreamed it could be. You are the leaders I wish I had when I started. This book was written for you and inspired by you. Thank you from the bottom of my heart.

To my HoneyBook family. Since 2015, HoneyBook has been filled with the dearest friends, mentors, and leaders, all of whom have given me the understanding of belonging as I know it now. To Oz and Naama

Alon for believing in the power of community. Your support over the past five years has transformed tens of thousands of lives—including mine. To Dan Visnick for your leadership, mentorship, and encouragement. To Kait Masters for making this community the best place that it can be. You are the leader that Rising Tide has always deserved. To Maria Povarchik for earning my friendship with your community-over-competition tattoo. We may live on different continents, but we're sisters all the same. To Austyn, LaShanta, Lauren, Olivia, and Wendy—thank you for pouring your heart and soul into Rising Tide over the years and for making it the community that it is today.

To the small but mighty NF team. To Bree Pair for being my right-hand woman throughout so much of this process. Thank you for fighting for this book right alongside me over the past two years, from the proposal through final publication. To Haylee Gaffin, who keeps our world spinning on its axis, thank you for all your hard work. To LaShonda Brown Delivuk for mobilizing our team of world changers and making this book launch a success.

To my literary agents, Karen, Curtis, and the entire Yates and Yates team. You believed in this book before a single word was ever written. You gave me the courage to take a risk that changed the course of my entire life. Thank you for using the gifts that God gave you to help others make their mark.

To the Worthy Publishing and Hachette team. Thank you for bringing this book to life. To Daisy for championing this project and amplifying my voice as a first-time author. To Karin for helping to edit this book into the best that it can be. To Patsy, Eliot, Katie, and Laini for using your brilliance to get this book into the hands of readers so that it could make an impact.

To Jennifer Duran of Pace Creative Design for using your genius to create the perfect cover for this book. You are a true artist and a talented designer.

To those who have shaped Rising Tide into a more diverse, inclusive, and equitable community—you are true heroes in the battle for belonging. To Nichole Alcántara Beiner Powell-Newman for spearheading our Equitable Leadership Training Program and for helping us to turn our aspired values into lived ones. To Kait Masters and Kit Gray for ensuring our chronically ill and disabled members will always have an honored seat at the table. To Kay Fabella for your invaluable leadership, perspective, and friendship. To Danait Berhe-Gaber for raising your hand and thereby raising the tide. To Dannie Lynn Fountain for your courage and your voice. To Lisette Cervano and Christian Gutierrez for leading the way and being fearless advocates. To Erin Perkins for relentlessly fighting for accessibility. To all members of the HoneyBook DEI team and to our community leaders past and present who have fought this fight, thank you.

To my mentors and teachers. To Dr. Gary Hatfield and Dr. Michael Leja, who helped me combine my love of art and science so that I could see the world with new eyes. To Laura Nestler for being the type of leader I will always aspire to be. To the St. Mary's, Archbishop Spalding, and University of Pennsylvania communities for investing in me and sparking my lifelong love of learning.

To my friends in San Francisco, Annapolis, and everywhere in between, who inspired so much of this book. To Rebecca Shostak for being the type of friend that I spent my whole life searching for. To Martha Bitar for convincing us to take the greatest risk of our lives and being a part of my story ever since. To Madison Short for supporting me—from building my photography business to the early days of Rising Tide to driving cross-country with us and our toddler. You are an extraordinary friend, and I love you. To Kent and Jami Heckel for saying yes to our wild adventures. To Reina Pomeroy for coaching me through roadblocks big and small. To Jessica Chang for showing me what it means to take care of the ones you love. To Abby Springmann for bold questions that brought me back to Jesus. To Lauren Swann for always letting me order the fried pickles. To Hope Taylor, Jennifer Ryals, Laylee Emadi Smith, Michelle Harris Templeton, and Vanessa Hicks for being the type of friends who feel like family. You mean more to me than you will ever know.

To the infertility warriors who taught me so much about the true meaning of community. Your courage made me brave. Your resilience made me strong. Thank you for being a light in one of the darkest seasons of my life.

To my family. Mom, thank you for everything. There are not enough pages in this book to adequately express how much I love you. You believed in me long before I ever believed in myself. Thank you for raising me to care deeply for others and value the importance of community. To my sister, Dr. Caroline Franke—you inspire me more than you will ever know. Thank you for assisting me with research as I set out to write this book. This world is a better place simply because you are in it.

To Mom-mom for bringing us all together and for watching over us still. I love you and miss you every single day. To my grandfather, Frank Pipkin, for teaching me the importance of faith and service to others. To see God through your eyes is to truly know Him. To my dad, Robin, my stepmother, Monica, and my little brother, Conor. I love you all so much. To the entire Pipkin crew—Mark, Karl, Stephanie, Matthew, Kate, and Christopher. Thank you for helping to shape me into the person that I am today. To Melissa, Hugh, Carter, Adriana. Thank you for raising the love of my life and for welcoming me into the Hayes family with open arms. To my son, Huey, you have changed me forever. Thank you for making me a mama.

And most important, to Jesus. You commanded us to love our neighbors and to put others before ourselves. My greatest hope is that throughout my life and my work, I do *precisely* that.

NOTES

CHAPTER 1

1. Cacioppo J. T., J. H. Fowler, and N.A. Christakis. "Alone in the Crowd: The Structure and Spread of Loneliness in a Large Social Network." *Journal of Personality and Social Psychology* 97, no. 6 (2009): 977–91. DOI:10.1037/a0016076.

2. Cacioppo J. T., and S. Cacioppo. "Older Adults Reporting Social Isolation or Loneliness Show Poorer Cognitive Function 4 Years Later." *Evidence-Based Nursing* 17, no. 2 (2014): 59–60. DOI: 10.1136/eb-2013-101379.

3. Holt-Lunstad, J., T. B. Smith, and J. B. Layton. "Social Relationships and Mortality Risk: A Meta-Analytic Review." *PLoS Medicine* 7 no. 7 (2010). DOI:10.1371/journal.pmed.1000316.

4. Winerman, Lea. "By the Numbers: An Alarming Rise in Suicide." *Monitor on Psychology* 50 no. 1. American Psychological Association, January 2019. https://www.apa.org/monitor/2019/01/numbers.

5. Gawande, Atul. "Hellhole: The United States Holds Tens of Thousands of Inmates in Long-Term Solitary Confinement. Is This Torture?" *New Yorker*, March 30, 2009. https://www.newyorker.com/magazine/2009/03/30/hellhole.

6. Senate Judiciary Subcommittee on the Constitution, Civil Rights, and Human Rights Hearing on Solitary Confinement. Testimony of Professor Craig Haney, June 19, 2012. https://www.judiciary.senate.gov/imo/media/doc/12-6-19HaneyTestimony.pdf.

7. McCain, John. "John McCain, Prisoner of War: A First-Person Account," *U.S. News & World Report*, January 28, 2008. https://www.usnews.com/news/articles/2008/01/28/john-mccain-prisoner-of-war-a-first-person-account.

8. Kozar, Richard, *John McCain* (Philadelphia, Chelsea House Publishers, 2002) 53.

9. Blanco-Suarez, Elena. "The Effects of Solitary Confinement on the Brain." *Psychology Today*, February 27, 2019. https://www.psychologytoday.com/us /blog/brain-chemistry/201902/the-effects-solitary-confinement-the-brain.

CHAPTER 2

1. Campbell, Benjamin. "A Neuroanthropological Perspective." *Evolutionary Anthropology* 21, no. 5 (2012):187. DOI:10.1002/evan.21328.

2. Buettner, D., S. Skemp. "Blue Zones: Lessons From the World's Longest Lived." *American Journal of Lifestyle Medicine* 10, no. 5 (2016): 318–321. DOI:10.1177/1559827616637066.

3. J. Holt-Lunstad, T. B. Smith, and J. B. Layton. "Social Relationships and Mortality Risk: A Meta-Analytic Review." *PLOS Medicine* 7, no. 7 (2010). DOI: 10.1371/journal.pmed.1000316.

4. *There is a decline in religious affiliation, even among those who were once raised in religious families.* (https://www.pewforum.org/2019/10/17/in-u-s-decline -of-christianity-continues-at-rapid-pace/); The number of adults attending club meetings has dropped significantly; *Fewer families are eating dinners together* (https://news.gallup.com/poll/10336/empty-seats-fewer-families -eat-together.aspx); *More and more people are living alone.* (https:// ourworldindata.org/living-alone).

CHAPTER 3

1. Musk, Elon. "All Our Patent Are Belong to You." *Tesla* (blog), June 12, 2014. https://www.tesla.com/blog/all-our-patent-are-belong-you.

CHAPTER 4

1. The Enneagram is a set of nine distinct personality types. You can learn more and find your type at the Enneagram Institute (https://www .enneagraminstitute.com/).

2. Costanzo, Linda S. *Physiology*. Fifth edition. Philadelphia, PA: Saunders, Elsevier, 2014. Print. Chapter 2: Autonomic Nervous System. Pages 45–64.

3. Triplett, N. "The Dynamogenic Factors in Pacemaking and Competition." *The American Journal of Psychology* 9 no. 4 (1898), 507–533. https://doi.org/10.2307/1412188.

4. Chen, S. "Social Modification of the Activity of Ants in Nest-Building." *Physiological Zoology* 10 no. 4 (1937): 420–36. https://doi.org/10.1086/physzool.10.4.30151428.

5. Rhea, Matthew R., Daniel M. Landers, Brent A. Alvar, and Shawn M. Arent. "The Effects of Competition and the Presence of an Audience on Weight Lifting Performance." *Journal of Strength and Conditioning Research* 17, no. 2 (2003): 303–6. https://doi.org/10.1519/00124278-200305000-00013.

6. *Online Etymology Dictionary*, s.v. "compete (v.)," accessed June 1, 2020, https://www.etymonline.com/word/compete.

7. "A Night to Remember," video file, 6:25, YouTube, posted by US Open Tennis Championships, September 1, 2019, https://www.youtube.com/watch?v=9zAqdVF489k; Maine, D'Arcy. "Naomi Osaka and Coco Gauff Teach a Lesson in Humility and Sportsmanship." ESPN. ESPN Internet Ventures, September 1, 2019. https://www.espn.com/tennis/story/_/id/27510249/naomi-osaka-coco-gauff-teach-lesson-humility-sportsmanship.

CHAPTER 5

1. Noor, Iqra. "Confirmation Bias." *Simple Psychology*, June 10, 2020. https://www.simplypsychology.org/confirmation-bias.html.

2. Brewer & Caporael, 2006; Navarrete, Kurzban, Fessler, & Kirkpatrick, 2004.

3. Stangor, Charles, Rajiv Jhangiani, and Hammond Tarry. "Ingroup Favoritism and Prejudice." Essay. In *Principles of Social Psychology*. Victoria: BCcampus Open Textbook Project, 2014. https://opentextbc.ca/socialpsychology/chapter/ingroup-favoritism-and-prejudice/.

4. Stangor, Charles, Rajiv Jhangiani, and Hammond Tarry. "Social Categorization and Stereotyping." Essay. In *Principles of Social Psychology*. Victoria: BCcampus Open Textbook Project, 2014. https://opentextbc.ca/socialpsychology/chapter/social-categorization-and-stereotyping/.

5. Hewstone, Miles, Frank Fincham, and Jos Jaspars. "Social Categorization and Similarity in Intergroup Behaviour: A Replication with 'Penalties.'" *European Journal of Social Psychology* 11, no. 1 (1981): 101–7. https://doi .org/10.1002/ejsp.2420110107; Locksley, Anne, Vilma Ortiz, and Christine Hepburn. "Social Categorization and Discriminatory Behavior: Extinguishing the Minimal Intergroup Discrimination Effect." *Journal of Personality and Social Psychology* 39, no. 5 (1980): 773–83. https://doi.org/10.1037/0022 -3514.39.5.773.

6. Stangor, Charles, Rajiv Jhangiani, and Hammond Tarry. "Ingroup Favoritism and Prejudice." Essay. In *Principles of Social Psychology*. Victoria: BCcampus Open Textbook Project, 2014. https://opentextbc.ca/socialpsychology /chapter/ingroup-favoritism-and-prejudice/.

CHAPTER 6

1. Heitner, Darren. "Watching Video Games Is Now Bigger Than Traditional Spectator Sporting Events." *Inc.*, April 2, 2018. https://www.inc.com/darren -heitner/watching-video-games-is-now-bigger-traditional-spectator-sporting -events.html.

2. Hunt, Melissa, Jordyn Young, Rachel Marx, and Courtney Lipson (2018). "No More FOMO: Limiting Social Media Decreases Loneliness and Depression." *Journal of Social and Clinical Psychology* 37. 751–768. 10.1521 /jscp.2018.37.10.751.

3. Primack BA, et al. "Social Media Use and Perceived Social Isolation Among Young Adults in the U.S." *Am J Prev Med.* 2017 Jul;53(1):1–8. doi: 10.1016/j.amepre.2017.01.010. Epub 2017 Mar 6. PMID: 28279545; PMCID: PMC5722463.

4. Vahedi, Zahra and Lilach Dahoah Halevi. (2019). "Social Networking Site Use and Self-Esteem: A Meta-Analytic Review." *Personality and Individual Differences* 153. doi: 10.1016/j.paid.2019.109639.

5 Cystic Fibrosis Foundation, *Infection Prevention and Control Clinical Care Guidelines.* https://www.cff.org/Care/Clinical-Care-Guidelines/Infection -Prevention-and-Control-Clinical-Care-Guidelines/Infection-Prevention -and-Control-Clinical-Care-Guidelines/.

CHAPTER 9

1. Walsh, Bari. "The Science of Resilience: Why Some Children Can Thrive Despite Adversity," March 23, 2015. https://www.gse.harvard.edu/news/uk/15/03/science-resilience.

CHAPTER 10

1. Nortje, Alicia. "Social Comparison: An Unavoidable Upward or Downward Spiral." PositivePsychology.com, September 1, 2020. https://positivepsychology.com/social-comparison/.
2. Wheeler, L., and K. Miyake. "Social Comparison in Everyday Life." *Journal of Personality and Social Psychology* 62 no. 5 (1992): 760–773. https://doi.org/10.1037/0022–3514.62.5.760.
3. Burton, Linda. "The Neuroscience of Gratitude: What You Need to Know about the New Neural Knowledge." https://www.whartonhealthcare.org/the_neuroscience_of_gratitude.

CHAPTER 11

1. Lin, Ying. "10 Reddit Statistics Every Marketer Should Know in 2020." *Oberlo* (blog), July 13, 2020. https://www.oberlo.com/blog/reddit-statistics.
2. Carmody, Dennis P., and Michael Lewis. "Brain Activation When Hearing One's Own and Others' Names." *Brain Research* 1116, no. 1 (2006): 153–158. https://doi.org/10.1016/j.brainres.2006.07.121.
3. Carnegie, Dale. *How to Win Friends and Influence People.* New York: Simon & Schuster, 1981.

CHAPTER 12

1. Parker, Priya. *The Art of Gathering: How We Meet and Why It Matters.* New York: Riverhead Books, 2018.

CHAPTER 13

1. vanOyen, W. C., T. E. Ludwig, and K. L. Vander Laan. "Granting Forgiveness or Harboring Grudges: Implications for Emotion, Physiology, and Health." *Psychological Science* 12, no. 2 (March 2001): 117–123. https://doi.org/10.1111/1467-9280.00320.

CHAPTER 14

1. Sprout Social. "#BrandsGetReal: What Consumers Want from Brands in a Divided Society." *Sprout Social* (blog), May 2, 2019. https://sproutsocial.com /insights/data/social-media-connection/.

2. Franke, Natalie. Interview with Douglas Atkin, Global Head of Community at Airbnb. Rising Tide Society Summit, December 8, 2015.

3. Airbnb. "Belong Anywhere." *Airbnb* (blog), July 18, 2014. https://blog .atairbnb.com/belong-anywhere/.

4. Passiak, David. "Belong Anywhere—The Vision and Story Behind Airbnb's Global Community." Medium. January 30, 2017. https://medium.com /cocreatethefuture/belong-anywhere-the-vision-and-story-behind-airbnbs -global-community-123d32218d6a.

5. Jones, Carrie. "How Udemy Increased their Instructor Engagement Rates by 4X using Facebook Groups." CMX, June 9, 2020. https://cmxhub.com /udemy-facebook-group-platform/.

6. Sephora's Community Hub. https://community.sephora.com/.

7. Ungerleider, Neal. "How Sephora Discovered That Lurkers Are Also Its 'Superfans.'" Fast Company, September 22, 2014. https://www.fastcompany .com/3035236/how-sephora-discovered-that-lurkers-are-also-its-superfans.

8. The Skimm. "Skim'bassadors." theSkimm. [December 13, 2020] https:// www.theskimm.com/general/skimmbassadors.

9. Gonzalez, Guadalupe. "Chewy's Co-Founder and Former CEO Explains How the Startup Went From Zero to an $8.7 Billion Public Company." Inc.com, June 14, 2019. https://www.inc.com/guadalupe-gonzalez/co-founder-ryan -cohen-what-makes-chewy-successful.html.

10. Agrawal, Radha. *Belong: Find Your People, Create Community, and Live a More Connected Life*. New York, New York: Workman Publishing, 2018.

11. Rozovsky, Julia. "The Five Keys to a Successful Google Team." re:Work. rework, November 17, 2015. https://rework.withgoogle.com/blog/five-keys -to-a-successful-google-team/.

12. Thread in Rising Tide Society Facebook group: https://www.facebook.com /groups/therisingtidesociety/permalink/1886804648309304/; "Fly Kyle to Texas for Stephanie!, Organized by Danielle Schamer." gofundme.com, May

23, 2017. https://www.gofundme.com/f/fly-kyle-to-texas-for-stephanie
?fbclid=IwAR24CZ0DAzAaoPDRKx91CIhS6oSAK6ucP7dAZ5S9NCKnfN
8WlRpAPTshJNM; Mahjouri, Shakiel. "Texas Girl Snags Date Of A Lifetime
To Ex's Wedding, 'Bachelorette Canada' Contestant Kyle Andrew Skinner."
ET Canada, May 24, 2017. https://etcanada.com/news/228047/texas-girl
-snags-date-of-a-lifetime-to-exs-wedding-bachelorette-canada-contestant
-kyle-andrew-skinner/.

READING GROUP GUIDE

CHAPTER 1: BUILT FOR BELONGING

"Cooperation and competition are a delicate balancing act wired directly into our genetic code. We are built to belong, and yet we are also created to compete. We are constantly at war with ourselves, and it doesn't take much for the balance of power to shift."

Why do you think the dichotomy between cooperation and competition exists? Why is it so difficult to overcome our tendency toward competition?

"In our pursuit of being *the* best, we lose sight of being *our* best. Slowly we trade interdependence for independence, we choose personal successes over the collective good, and we begin to believe the narrative that it is us versus them."

Discuss the difference between interdependence and independence. What are the pros and cons of each?

CHAPTER 2: MODERN TIMES, MODERN PROBLEMS

"When we are young, we learn about taking turns, sharing, getting along, encouraging others, and being kind; however, as we grow older, a slight shift occurs, and 'winning' becomes more of a priority."

What do you think are the reasons behind this shift? Can you identify when it took place in your own life?

"To fill the void that loneliness leaves in our hearts, we confuse consumption with connection."

What are the dangers of confusing consumption with connection?

CHAPTER 3: THE RISING TIDE

"A rising tide lifts all boats."

Discuss this idea. What are some ways we can retrain our brains to view our competitors as those who can also do the most to support us and lift us up?

"All relationships—personal or professional—succeed or fail based on that simple principle: *How do you make people feel? Does each interaction feel transactional or relational?*"

People remember how you treat them and how you make them feel. Why do you think we've become a society in which transactional interactions are more common or more respected than relational ones?

CHAPTER 4: PEOPLE FIRST, OPPORTUNITY SECOND

"If someone else won a race in the short term, it didn't mean that I lost in the long term."

Why do you think we've been conditioned to believe that if someone else wins it means we lose? How can we challenge that idea?

"What if by simply being in the arena with someone else, you could be better at whatever it is that you do? Psychologists refer to this phenomenon as "social facilitation," and they have been studying it since the close of the nineteenth century."

Discuss the concept of social facilitation and how we can use it not to try to beat our competitors but to improve upon our *own* abilities?

CHAPTER 5: MASTERING OUR MINDSETS

"We have a tendency to prefer and respond more favorably to people who are members of our own social group through a practice known as ingroup favoritism. Additionally, we tend to see people who belong to the same social group as more similar than they are in reality, and we tend to judge people from different social groups as more different from us than they are in reality."

What are some of the downfalls of only associating with people who are similar to us? What kinds of enriching relationships are we missing out on when we refuse to expand beyond our own circle?

"Wherever there are limited resources, albeit objectively scarce or perceived to be scarce, humans shift from being open and altruistic to self-preserving and self-serving."

Where is the false narrative in this idea? In our communities, where is there abundance to be found where we once believed there was scarcity?

CHAPTER 6: DIGITAL TOGETHERNESS

"There is a difference between enabling social media to be a gateway for comparison and empowering yourself to use it as a vehicle for deep connection."

What are some ways that social media and technology are causing us to be more disconnected from one another than ever before? Conversely, what are some ways that social media can be a useful tool (used responsibly) for building authentic community and creating genuine connection across the world?

"Seeking to understand the online and offline integration of our lives requires us to identify the ways in which these worlds are woven together, thereby forcing us to intentionally seek out better ways to leverage technology for the benefit of ourselves and others."

In many ways, interaction with technology and social media in some form is unavoidable in our twenty-first-century society. How do we then manage our use of it in healthy ways? How can we use it to our advantage and not let it control us?

CHAPTER 7: *VULNERABILITY* IS NOT A BUZZWORD

"I had to surrender my sense of normalcy and relinquish my perception of control without a clear end in sight."

Have you ever had to do this? What was that experience like? What did you learn from it?

"Along the way, I've learned that vulnerability isn't a destination. There is no arriving, only becoming."

Discuss this idea. Why is it important to be vulnerable with others in your community?

CHAPTER 8: FITTING IN IS OVERRATED

"In the process of growing up, we trade an innocent confidence in who we are for a fear about what makes us inadequate or different in the eyes of others."

What are some ways we can fight back against this trend? How can we raise the next generation to maintain that confidence and sense of worth throughout their lives?

"Sometimes we overlook what we have to offer this world because we fail to see the extraordinary in what we've been conditioned to believe is ordinary."

What are some areas of your life that you've begun to view as "ordinary" that are actually quite extraordinary?

CHAPTER 9: STRONGEST IN THE STRUGGLE

"In order to strengthen our resilience, we must be open and willing to tear down those narratives that tell us to go at it alone. We must open our eyes to the outstretched arms all around us. We must be willing to give and to accept help."

Why is this so hard, and why could this feel counterintuitive?

"So often we think of relationships as something that stems from seasons of prosperity, but I truly believe that community is strongest in the struggle. It is strengthened by shared experience and is designed to be our safe place to land."

Why is it especially necessary to surround ourselves with a strong community during our season of struggle, even when we might feel like pulling away?

CHAPTER 10: OVERCOMING COMPARISON

"Comparison isn't just the thief of joy—it's the plunderer of purpose, the burglar of belonging."

What are some ways that we can break free from the comparison trap?

"The underlying truth is that social comparison is a hardwired part of the human experience and in its simplest form is an innate act of self-evaluation. In order to understand how we are performing in life, our brain looks to others as a benchmark."

To a certain extent, comparing and evaluating ourselves to others is a natural part of our self-evaluation—but it's a fine line. When can comparison become more harmful than helpful?

CHAPTER 11: FINDING YOUR PEOPLE

"Sometimes we cannot quite envision how our lives will change when we disrupt our daily routine to try something new."

When has this been true in your own life? How has your life changed since you disrupted your usual habits? What are some ways you can get out of your comfort zone right now?

"When you step into your search for community unsure of who you are and weighed down by insecurities, you're more likely to change yourself to fit in rather than seeking a place where you are accepted for who you truly are."

Are there any safeguards you could put in place to help recognize when you may be tempted to change yourself to better fit within a community?

CHAPTER 12: COMMUNITY BUILDING 101

"A community is only as great as its leaders. The leaders of your community will directly shape the culture and the way members feel as they join and engage in the organization."

What are some qualities and skills that you admire in leaders? How can you foster those ideals in yourself and members of your community/organization?

"We have control over the traditions that we are a part of in our lives and communities. We do not need to repeat traditions that no longer serve us. We can create new ones that are in deeper alignment with our purpose."

Choose a tradition that you participate in to analyze. Is it still positively serving its purpose and bringing meaningful experiences to those involved? What could new or updated traditions look like?

CHAPTER 13: REJECTION AND REDEMPTION

"As humans, we are imperfect beings. Even with pure intentions, we are capable of causing harm. Even when we strive to create spaces of belonging, we run the risk of doing the opposite."

What are some ways, both positive and negative, that you have handled rejection in the past? What did you learn from that experience?

"Forgiving doesn't mean forgetting. Forgiving means moving forward, and it is a profound gift that we give to ourselves."

Forgiveness is something that a lot of people struggle with, even when the result is positive. Why do you think this is? Where are these incorrect definitions of forgiveness coming from?

CHAPTER 14: THE TRUE ROI OF COMMUNITY

"Behind every successful human being is a person or people who introduced them to their power and potential. Connection and collaboration are the keys to developing into the people we were always meant to be."

Ask these questions while thinking over your own life: *Who affirmed your self-esteem and built your confidence? Who nurtured your resilience and modeled perseverance in your life? Who sacrificed for you? Who still sacrifices for you?*

"Hardships big and small are solved by the collective efforts of the community. People helping people, ensuring that no one has to face this life alone."

What are some ways that you can enthusiastically rally around those in your life?

ABOUT THE AUTHOR

Natalie Franke is one of the founders of the Rising Tide Society—a community of over 70,000 creative entrepreneurs who gather in more than 400 cities around the world in the spirit of community over competition. She took a hashtag (#communityovercompetition) and turned it into a movement and a vibrant community that now spans the globe. Natalie currently lives in Annapolis, Maryland, with her husband and son and serves as the Head of Community for HoneyBook and Rising Tide, leading a team of world changers in the pursuit of empowering the creative economy to rise together doing what they love.